THE SOCIAL
WORKOUT BOOK

TITLES OF RELATED INTEREST FROM PINE FORGE PRESS

Adventures in Social Research: Data Analysis Using SPSS® for Windows™ by Earl Babbie and Fred Halley

Social Work in the 21st Century by Eileen Gambrill and Michael Reisch

Critical Thinking for Social Workers: A Workbook by Leonard Gibbs and Eileen Gambrill

Exploring Social Issues Using SPSS® for Windows™ by Joseph R. Healey, Earl Babbie, and Fred Halley

Race, Ethnicity, Gender, and Class: The Sociology of Group Conflict and Change by Joseph F. Healey

Race, Ethnicity, and Gender in the United States: Inequality, Group Conflict, and Power by Joseph F. Healey

Aging: Concepts and Controversies, 2nd edition, by Harry R. Moody

Building Community: Social Science in Action edited by Philip Nyden, Anne Figert, Mark Shibley, and Darryl Burrows

Diversity in America by Vincent Parrillo

Shifts in the Social Contract: Understanding Change in American Society by Beth A. Rubin

Worlds of Difference: Inequality in the Aging Experience, 2nd edition, by Eleanor Palo Stoller and Rose Campbell Gibson

Community Resources for Older Adults: Programs and Services in an Era of Change by Robbyn Wacker and Karen Roberto

---

The Pine Forge Press Series in Research Methods and Statistics
Edited by Kathleen S. Crittenden

Regression: A Primer by Paul Allison

A Guide to Field Research by Carol A. Bailey

Designing Surveys: A Guide to Decisions and Procedures by Ronald Czaja and Johnny Blair

Social Statistics for a Diverse Society by Chava Frankfort-Nachmias

Experimental Design and the Analysis of Variance by Robert Leik

How Sampling Works by Richard Maisel and Caroline Hodges Persell

Program Evaluation by George McCall

Investigating the Social World: The Process and Practice of Research by Russell K. Schutt

THE SOCIAL WORKOUT BOOK

Strength-Building Exercises for the Pre-Professional

ALICE A. LIEBERMAN
University of Kansas

Pine Forge Press
Thousand Oaks, California • London • New Delhi

For information:

 Pine Forge Press
A Sage Publications Company
2455 Teller Road
Thousand Oaks, California 91320
sales@pfp.sagepub.com

SAGE Publications Ltd.
6 Bonhill Street
London EC2A 4PU
United Kingdom

SAGE Publications India Pvt. Ltd.
M-32 Market
Greater Kailash I
New Delhi 110 048 India

Production Editor: Sanford Robinson
Production Coordinator: Windy Just
Copy Editor: Joyce Kuhn
Production Assistant: Karen Wiley
Designer/Typesetter: Rebecca Evans
Cover: Ravi Balasuriya
Print Buyer: Anna Chin

Printed in the United States of America

00 01 02 03 10 9 8 7 6 5 4 3

Library of Congress Cataloging-in-Publication Data

Lieberman, Alice A.
    The social workout book: Strength-building exercises for the
pre-professional / by Alice A. Lieberman.
        p.   cm.
    Includes bibliographical references and index.
    ISBN 0-7619-8531-X (alk. paper)
    1. Social work education—United States.   I. Title.
HV11.L48 1997
361.3'2'071073—dc21   97-33799

ABOUT THE AUTHOR

Alice A. Lieberman, PhD, LMSW, is Associate Professor and Chair of the Baccalaureate Program in the School of Social Welfare at the University of Kansas, Lawrence. She has taught at both BSW and MSW levels for 15 years. Her professional experience includes clinical work in a large metropolitan hospital, a small family service agency, and administrative work at a small voluntary agency. She has written numerous articles, book chapters, and book reviews that focus generally on the impact of legislative and policy changes on access to services by the profession's traditional client base. The author welcomes comments from you, the consumer of this book. Please direct your comments by E-mail to: alicel@ukans.edu

ABOUT THE PUBLISHER

Pine Forge Press is a new educational publisher, dedicated to publishing innovative books and software throughout the social sciences. On this and any other of our publications, we welcome your comments and suggestions.

Please call or write to:

Pine Forge Press
A Sage Publications Company
2455 Teller Road
Thousand Oaks, California 91320

(805) 499-4224

FAX (805) 499-7881

E-mail: sales@pfp.sagepub.com

Visit our new World Wide Web site, your direct link to a multitude of on-line resources:

http://www.sagepub.com/pineforge

To Ethan and Jared

BRIEF OUTLINE

Acknowledgments xiii

Introduction xv

1 SOCIAL WELFARE: HISTORY, POLITICS, POLICIES, AND SERVICES

WORKOUT 1
Appreciating the Living History of Social Work 3

WORKOUT 2
Learning From the Social Work Community 13

WORKOUT 3
Debating Contemporary Issues in Social Welfare 19

WORKOUT 4
Budgeting a Poverty-Level Income 27

WORKOUT 5
Influencing Local Public Policy 35

2 THE SOCIAL WORK PROFESSION

WORKOUT 6
Understanding Social Work Regulation in Your State 43

WORKOUT 7
Using the Internet to Enhance Professional Socialization 51

WORKOUT 8
Shaping Public Perception of Social Work 57

WORKOUT 9
Clarifying Your Values 65

WORKOUT 10
Examining the Impact of Religious Values on the Clients of Social Work 71

WORKOUT 11
Helping Clients Formulate Identity: Homosexuality 79

WORKOUT 12
Leading Clients From Oppression to Empowerment 85

3 THE PRACTICE OF SOCIAL WORK

WORKOUT 13
Assessing Clients' Strengths   147

WORKOUT 14
Illuminating Research: Participant Observation   157

WORKOUT 15
Acquiring Goods and Services for Clients:
Resource Acquisition   163

4 A VISION FOR THE FUTURE

WORKOUT 16
Caring for the Elderly in the 21st Century   175

WORKOUT 17
Envisioning the Future of Social Work   181

Bibliography   187

Index   189

CONTENTS

Acknowledgments   xiii

Introduction   xv

1 SOCIAL WELFARE: HISTORY, POLITICS, POLICIES, AND SERVICES

WORKOUT 1

Appreciating the Living History of Social Work (in or outside class)   3

You are asked to read and interpret the writings of an early leader in social welfare. Do her words sound like those of any of today's policymakers or politicians?

WORKOUT 2

Learning From the Social Work Community (outside class)   13

This Workout provides you with an opportunity to learn more about an event in the history of the social work community from people with first-hand knowledge. The skills required for this Workout include honing a research question, interviewing, and interpreting the data you receive from your source.

WORKOUT 3

Debating Contemporary Issues in Social Welfare (in and outside class)   19

Social workers need to possess the skills of articulation and persuasion if they wish to influence public debate on issues of importance to their clients. How do your skills measure up?

WORKOUT 4

Budgeting a Poverty-Level Income (in and outside class)   27

Across the country, debate rages about the adequacy of benefits in income maintenance programs. Perceptions of what it takes to live in even margin-ally adequate style in the United States vary widely. How would you con-struct a minimally adequate budget for a family? This Workout requires you to think critically and to be amenable to compromise with peers.

WORKOUT 5

Influencing Local Public Policy (in class or E-mail)   35

What are the local issues currently being debated in your town, and how will their resolution impact those populations with whom social workers have historically been concerned? For example, are budget recisions threat-ening cuts in programs for disadvantaged youth? Are developers "gentrify-ing" low-income neighborhoods, and contributing to the displacement of residents? Is your city considering changes in its hiring practices that would have some impact on potential clients (e.g., relaxing affirmative action poli-cies, or hiring welfare recipients)? This Workout will get you off the side-lines and into the dialogue!

2 **THE SOCIAL WORK PROFESSION**

WORKOUT 6

Understanding Social Work Regulation in Your State (in and outside class)   43

At the present time, all states have some statutes on the books that regulate the practice of social work. These regulations address such questions who may call themselves social worker as, the tasks a social worker can and/or cannot do, and the like. It is important for you to know the regulatory parameters of your state (and how it differs from other states). Equally important, you need to decide whether licensure, certification, or registration is ultimately a plus for the profession and its clients.

WORKOUT 7

Using the Internet to Enhance Professional Socialization (outside class)   51

How might your proficiency with the Internet help you in both your social work education and practice? What kinds of resources are available to you on the Internet? Does this method of retrieving information pose any distinct advantages over more traditional means? Find out here!

WORKOUT 8

Shaping Public Perception of Social Work (outside class)   57

What does the popular press (such as mainstream newspapers and magazines) have to say about social work and social workers? How does television portray the profession? Like it or not, the world views social work and social workers largely through these dual prisms. Are they accurate?

WORKOUT 9

Clarifying Your Values (in class)   65

With the exception of the clergy, the social work profession is the most value-based of all. Thus, if you are contemplating entering this profession, a full examination of your personal values is a prerequisite.

WORKOUT 10

Examining the Impact of Religious Values on the Clients
of Social Work (in and outside class)   71

This Workout builds on the previous one. For many of us, religious belief constitutes the foundation of our personal values. Yet, some of those values may conflict with those of our clients. How do we reconcile religious tenets with the values inherent in our practice and in the social policies we work with?

WORKOUT 11

Helping Clients Formulate Identity: Homosexuality (in and outside class)   79

The formulation of identity—and the assertion of that identity to the world—are important developmental tasks. A person's ability to confidently take on these tasks may be seriously impaired if his or her identity—or some aspect of who that person is—is stigmatized in society at large. How would you proclaim your identity to those closest to you if you thought that such self-disclosure might mean disappointment at best or rejection and isolation at worst?

WORKOUT 12

Leading Clients From Oppression to Empowerment
(in class, with outside preparation time)   85

Many of our clients have experienced discrimination and oppression based on their race or ethnicity, their mental or physical condition, or their dependent status. To help you understand their point of view, this Workout presents several instructive writings: *Impressions of an Indian Girlhood, The*

School Days of an Indian Girl, and *A Teacher Among Indians* by Zitkala-Sa, plus excerpts from *An Unquiet Mind* by Kay Redfield Jamison, *This Boy's Life* by Tobias Wolff, *Waist-High in the World* by Nancy Mairs, and *Lakota Woman* by Mary Crow Dog.

3 THE PRACTICE OF SOCIAL WORK

WORKOUT 13
Assessing Clients' Strengths (in class)   147

Human beings are socialized to focus on their problems and to overcome them. How would our lives, and the lives of our clients, be different if instead we focused upon clients' strengths—their abilities, resources, talents, and skills—as a way of helping them get their needs met?

WORKOUT 14
Illuminating Research: Participant Observation (in and outside class)   157

If we are to come to any profound understanding of the way people live their lives, we should be able to put ourselves, if only for a short time "in another's shoes." Maybe you have lived in low-income housing or known the feeling of food scarcity. If so, you may be familiar with the experience we try to engender in this exercise. But whether you have or have not, the structure of this Workout will provide you with a sense of the skills required to learn more about the experiences of others.

WORKOUT 15
Acquiring Goods and Services for Clients:
Resource Acquisition (outside class)   163

What kinds of services are available for clients with a variety of needs in your community? Where are the resource gaps? What are the problems that social workers encounter as they try to meet the various needs of their clients? You can find out by completing this Workout.

4 A VISION FOR THE FUTURE

WORKOUT 16
Caring for the Elderly in the 21st Century (in and outside class)   175

By 2020, approximately 20% of the U.S. population will be over the age of 65. Furthermore, people are living longer and so are spending ever-increasing proportions of their lives in this age category. The quality of life that you will have when you are old depends very much on how you prepare for older age now. What are you doing to prepare for your old age? What services and income supports should be available for the elderly now and in the future? This Workout helps you think about these things.

WORKOUT 17
Envisioning the Future of Social Work (in class)   181

Managed care, privatization, the Internet, and other "new information technologies" are having a profound impact on the social work profession, the services we provide for clients, and the policies guiding the distribution of those services. Yet none of these phenomena were part of our world 15 or 20 years ago. How visionary are you? What do you think the world of social work and social welfare will look like in the new milennium?

Bibliography   187

Index   189

ACKNOWLEDGMENTS

This book is the product of many hands and minds. To the following people who labored over this project by reading and providing critical feedback, you have my grateful thanks: Steve Rutter at Pine Forge Press (who, unbelievably, never got overtly angry about those missed deadlines); my longtime friend and editor of this series, Jeff Edleson; Jean Skeels, Windy Just, and Sanford Robinson, Pine Forge Press; Kimberly Strom-Gottfried (call your agent!); and the following extremely helpful reviewers, who waded through previous drafts:

David L. Burton, University of Michigan

Marjorie Donovan, Pittsburg State University

George Gottfried, College of St. Benedict

Nancy Keeton, Brescia College

Eunice McDowell, University of Oklahoma

Jane Reeves, Virginia Commonwealth University

Jim Wolk, Georgia State University

Thanks also to Le-Thu Tuttle, who provided technical support.

I would also like to thank my husband, Tom McDonald, our children, Ethan and Jared, my wonderful friends and colleagues here at the University of Kansas, the Baccalaureate Program Directors (BPD), who provided online support in the initial stages of this project, and the IPE.

The author wishes to express her gratitude to those writers and publishers who kindly granted permission to reprint the material noted below:

NASW Press for permission to reproduce, on pages 3 to 6, "The Working Definition of Social Work Practice," by Harriet M. Bartlett. *Social Work 3*(2), 3-9, 1958. Copyright © 1958, National Association of Social Workers, Inc., *Social Work*.

Alfred A Knopf Inc. for permission to reprint on pages 104-106 an excerpt from *An Unquiet Mind* by Kay Redfield Jamison. Copyright © by Kay Redfield Jamison.

Tobias Wolff and Grove/Atlantic, Inc., for permission to reprint on pages 106 to 108 an excerpt from *This Boy's Life* by Tobias Wolff. Copyright © 1989 by Tobias Wolff.

Beacon Press, Boston, for permission to reprint on pages 108 to 117 an excerpt from *Waist-High in the World* by Nancy Mairs. Copyright © 1996 by Nancy Mairs.

Grove/Atlantic, Inc. for permission to reprint on pages 117 to 134 excerpts from *Lakota Woman* by Mary Crow Dog and Richard Erdoes. Copyright © 1990 by Mary Crow Dog and Richard Erdoes.

INTRODUCTION

Welcome to *The Social WorkOut Book*. Whether you are committed to a social welfare major, undecided about your future career goals, or enrolled in this course simply to satisfy your curiosity, I think you will enjoy and learn a great deal from these "workouts" about social welfare and the profession charged with carrying out its mission, social work.

Although each workout is designed to meet a specific purpose, taken together they meet several overarching goals:

- To provide you with "hands-on" experience in the application of knowledge and skills central to basic social work and social policy practice.
- To help you increase your understanding of the context in which services are provided.
- To assist you in articulating your own personal value system and helping you to develop a framework for examining human problems that integrates both your personal values and the values of the profession.

In other words, I want you to develop and use your social work "muscles" so that by the end of this course you will have even greater enthusiasm for this profession and greater certainty about your own future as a social worker. Conversely, should you decide as a result of this course that social work and you are not as good a match as you might have hoped, that too, is a positive outcome as you can then focus your energies on other potential career paths. For those who fall into this latter category, this book should nevertheless help build your respect for the widely varied and often very difficult work that social workers do.

HOW TO USE THIS BOOK

This book is intended for use in any pre-professional introductory class in baccalaureate programs in social work and social welfare. But it is not written specifically for any one of these, and so the order of the Workouts may not necessarily follow the presentation of content in the primary textbook you use. I expect and hope that you and your instructor will skip around, using the Workouts to illuminate content as it is covered.

Each workout begins with a **prologue** that provides a context for the work you are about to begin and gives you any conceptual information you might need. The workout then articulates the **location** where the exercise is to be done (in class, outside class, or a combination, for those workouts that require outside preparation for presentation to the class). This "where" information is followed by a brief description of the **purpose**(s) of the workout, the background, and the directions for successfully completing it. Read the **directions** through carefully before proceeding with the full workout. Ask your instructor for assistance if there is anything you do not understand. The workout concludes with templates that are, in effect, your **workspace**. The perforations along the sides of the pages allow you to easily tear those pages out and hand them in.

Of course, your instructor may wish to modify an assignment. In addition, some of the workouts may require some preparatory work on the part of your instructor. Thus, you would be well advised to wait until a particular Workout has been assigned and discussed by your instructor before undertaking the effort.

Why do people work out? They usually want to build muscles, get rid of fat, and lose weight. But there is also considerable evidence that working out improves general health, reduces stress, and gives people a greater sense of their endurance potential and, in doing so, fosters a sense of well-being. By the end of this semester, after using this book, you should be able to reduce any stress and uncertainty you may have about entering this profession and should begin to develop strong "social work" muscles.

Have a great workout!

I

SOCIAL WELFARE
History, Politics, Policies, and Services

WORKOUT 1 Appreciating the Living History of Social Work

The history of social work is filled with vibrance, excitement, struggle, and change. Heavily influenced by such historical events as the waves of immigrants coming to our shores at the turn of the century, the two world wars, the Great Depression, the War on Poverty, and the continuing struggles for civil rights for oppressed minorities and women, social work continues both to respond to historical events and to proactively grow and change.

The primary texts assigned to you by your instructor discuss the history of our profession at considerable length. Most begin with the development of the competing ideas of Jane Addams and Mary Richmond. The former, the founder (along with Florence Kelly and Ellen Gates Starr) of Hull House, is credited with establishing the social reform movement in social work. Her belief that problems resulted from environmental deficiencies was in stark contrast to Richmond's, the prime mover behind the Charity Organization Society, which promulgated, through its "friendly visitor" program, the idea that problems are a result of interpersonal deficiencies that can only be cured through moral betterment. Eventually (and with significant assistance from Freud), Richmond's view gained greater acceptance, and although the profession has evolved significantly and become more secular than Richmond's views would suggest, her influence is still felt.

It is quite difficult to imagine what social work was like back in those days, but a visit to some of the museums and archives around the country provide fascinating insights. For example, if you ever have the chance, visit the Smithsonian Institution of American History, where the exhibit "From Parlor to Politics: Women and Social Reform" is on permanent display. This exhibit, which details the social activism of African American women, mothers of sons in war, and the social reformers of Hull House, made me very proud of my professional ancestors. Similarly, a visit to Ellis Island in New York City allows you to see a bit of the role social workers played in assisting immigrants coming to their new home (one of their roles, believe it or not, was to apply cosmetics to the women who were getting off the boats to meet their future husbands for the first time. If the prospective husband found his prospective bride unappealing, she had to go back, so she wanted to look as good as she could!).

Although Schools of Social Work were developing on campuses in the early 1900s, it was not until 1955 that the National Association of Social Workers was formed and our major professional journal *Social Work* began to be published. And it was not until 1958 that the working definition for social work practice, which we still operate from today, was published in those pages.

WORKING DEFINITION OF SOCIAL WORK PRACTICE

Social work practice, like the practice of all professions, is recognized by a constellation of value, purpose, sanction, knowledge, and method. No part alone is characteristic of social work practice nor is any part described here unique to social work. It is the particular content and configuration of this constellation that makes it social work practice and distinguishes it from the practice of other professions. The following is an attempt to spell out the components of this constellation in such a way as to include all social work practice with all its specializations. This implies that some social work practice will show a more extensive use of one or the other of the components but it is social work practice only when they are all present to some degree.

Value

Certain philosophical concepts are basic to the practice of social work:

1. The individual is the primary concern of this society.
2. There is interdependence among individuals in this society.
3. They have social responsibility for one another.
4. There are human needs common to each person, yet each person is essentially unique and different from others.
5. An essential attribute of a democratic society is the realization of the full potential of each individual and the assumption of his social responsibility through active participation in society.
6. Society has a responsibility to provide ways in which obstacles to this self-realization (i.e., disequilibrium between the individual and his environment) can be overcome or prevented.

These concepts provide the philosophical foundation for social work practice.

Purpose

The practice of social work has as its purposes the following:

1. Assist individuals and groups to identify and resolve or minimize problems arising out of disequilibrium between themselves and their environment.
2. Identify potential areas of disequilibrium between individuals or groups and the environment to prevent the occurrence of disequilibrium.
3. Seek out, identify, and strengthen the maximum potential in individuals, groups, and communities.

Sanction (i.e., authoritative permission; countenance, approbation, or support)

Social work has developed out of a community recognition of the need to provide services to meet basic needs, services that require the intervention of practitioners trained to understand the services, themselves, the individuals, and the means for bringing all together. Social work is not practiced in a vacuum or at the choice of its practitioners alone. Thus, there is a social responsibility inherent in the practitioner's role for the way in which services are rendered. The authority and power of practitioners and what they represent to the clients and group members derive from one or a combination of three sources:

1. *Governmental agencies* or their subdivisions (authorized by law)
2. *Voluntary incorporated agencies,* which have taken responsibility for meeting certain needs or providing certain services necessary for individual and group welfare
3. The *organized profession,* which in turn can sanction individuals for the practice of social work and set forth the educational and other requirements for practice and the conditions under which that practice may be undertaken, whether or not carried out under organizational auspices

Knowledge

Social work, like all other professions, derives knowledge from a variety of sources and in application brings forth further knowledge from its own processes. Since people's knowledge is never final or absolute, social workers in their application of this knowledge take into account those phenomena that are exceptions to existing generalizations and are aware and ready to deal with the spontaneous and unpredictable in human behavior. The practice of the social worker is typically guided by knowledge of the following:

1. Human development and behavior characterized by emphasis on the wholeness of individuals and the reciprocal influences of people and their total environment—human, social, economic, and cultural
2. The psychology of giving and taking help from another person or source outside the individual
3. Ways in which people communicate with one another and give outer expression to inner feelings, such as words, gestures, and activities
4. Group process and the efforts of groups upon individuals and the reciprocal influence of individuals on the group
5. The meaning and effect on the individual, groups, and community of cultural heritage including its religious beliefs, spiritual values, laws, and other social institutions
6. Relationships—the interactional processes between individuals, between individuals and groups, and between groups
7. The community—its internal processes, modes of development and change, its social services, and resources
8. The social services—their structure, organization, and method
9. The self, which enables individual practitioners to be aware of and to take responsibility for their own emotions and attitudes as these affect their professional functions

Method (i.e., an orderly systematic model of procedure; as used here, the term encompasses social casework, social group work, and community organization)

The social work method is the responsible, conscious, disciplined use of self in a relationship with an individual or group. Through this relationship practitioners facilitate interaction between individuals and their social environment with a continuing awareness of the reciprocal effects of one upon the other. It facilitates change within (1) the individual in relation to his or her social environment; (2) the social environment in its effect upon the individual; and (3) both the individual and the social environment in their interaction.

Social work method includes systematic observation and assessment of the individual or group in a situation and the formulation of an appropriate plan of action. Implicit in this is a continuing evaluation regarding the nature of the relationships between worker and client or group, and its effect on both the participant individual or group and the worker himself. This evaluation provides the basis for the professional judgment that workers must constantly make and that determines the direction of their activities. The method is used predominantly in interviews, group sessions, and conferences.

Techniques (i.e., instruments or tools used as a part of method). Incorporated in the use of the social work method may be one or more of the following techniques in different combinations: (1) support, (2) clarification, (3) information giving, (4) interpretation, (5) development of insight, (6) differentiation of the social worker from the individual or group, (7) identification with agency function, (8) creation and use of structure, (9) use of activities and projects, (10) provision of positive experiences, (11) teaching, (12) stimulation of group interaction, (13) limit setting, (14) utilization of available social resources, (15) effecting change in immediate environmental forces operating upon the individual or groups, and/or (16) synthesis.

Skill (i.e., technical expertness; the ability to use knowledge effectively and readily in execution or performance). Competence in social work practice lies in developing skill in the use of the method and its techniques described above. This means the ability to help particular clients or groups in such a way that they clearly understand the social worker's intention and role and are able to participate in the process of solving their problems. Setting the stage, the strict observance of confidentiality, encouragement, stimulation or participation, empathy, and objectivity are means of facilitating communication. Individual social workers always make their own creative contribution in the application of social work method to any setting or activity.

As a way of increasing skill and providing controls to the activity of the social work practitioner, the following are used: (1) recording, (2) supervision, (3) case conferences, (4) consultation, and (5) review and evaluation.

Teaching, Research, and Administration

Three important segments of social work—namely, teaching, research, and administration—have significance for the development, extension, and transmission of knowledge of social work practice. These have many elements in common with social work practice but also have their own uniqueness and some different objectives.

WORKOUT 1 *Instructions*

Location

In or outside class

Purpose

1. To provide you with a sense of the professional history that all social workers have in common and the ways it resonates in the present.
2. To provide you with experience in reading original documents.

Background

To gain a more profound sense of our history and to be able to judge it in the context of current developments in social work and social welfare, it is necessary to turn to primary sources. Included here are the words of one of the profession's most important figures, Josephine Shaw Lowell. Lowell never gained the fame of Jane Addams, yet reading her words, it is interesting to think about how her experiences shaped our profession. Lowell brought a somewhat different perspective to social work than many of our other professional forebears.

Lowell was one of the founders of the Charity Organization Society of New York and a leader in the movement in the United States to reorganize public and private charities in accordance with the principles of "scientific philanthrophy." Her greatest contributions include the instigation of many notable reforms such as increasing the number of institutions for the insane, state reformatories for women, and asylums for "feeble-minded" women. She deeply believed in the cause of wage and working-hour regulation for women, whom she saw shamelessly exploited; she also championed women's suffrage and civil service reform. Although she was widowed very early in life, her three sisters, all of whom married men who were in public service, were supportive of her work (and of her) throughout her life.

Directions

1. Read the following excerpt from a speech by Lowell, recorded in the *Proceedings of the National Conference of Charities and Corrections* (Lowell, 1890/1997). The piece reflects her thoughts on the effects of social welfare. Over a century later, this remains a timely subject.
2. After reading the piece, answer the questions in the Workout 1 Workspace.

The Economic and Moral Effects of Public Outdoor Relief

by Mrs. Charles Russell [Josephine Shaw] Lowell, of New York

I have not been able to assent to the report of the Chairman of the Committee on Indoor and Outdoor Relief, only because, as it seems to me, it does not draw the distinction which is necessary between public and private relief.

I admit, of course, that there are persons who need relief (that is, *help*) with their own homes, and that both Pitt's argument and Mr. Sanborn's argument apply to such: "Great care should be taken, in relieving their distresses, not to throw them into the great class of vagrant and homeless poor." Such people, however, are to my mind, not proper subjects for relief at all; for what is public relief, and upon what grounds is it to be justified? Public relief is money paid by the bulk of the community (every community is of course composed mainly of those who are working hard to obtain a livelihood) to certain members of the community; not, however, voluntarily or spontaneously by those interested in the individuals receiving it, but paid by public officers from money raised by taxation. The justification for the expenditure of public money (money raised by taxation) is that it is necessary for the public good. That certain persons need certain things is no reason for supplying them with those things from the public funds. Before this can be rightly done, it is necessary to prove that it is good for the community at large that it should be done . . .

The practice of any community in this particular is a matter of great importance, for there can be no question that there is an inverse ratio between the welfare of the mass of the people and the distribution of relief. What some one has called "the fatal ease of living without work and the terrible difficulty of living by work" are closely interrelated as cause and effect; and if you will permit me, I will try to show by a short allegory what this relation is.

Once upon a time there lived in a valley, called the Valley of Industry, a people who were happy and industrious. All the goods of this life were applied to them by exhaustless subterranean springs of water, which they pumped up into a great reservoir on the top of a neighboring hill, the Hill of Prosperity, from which it flowed down, each man receiving what he himself pumped up, by a small pipe which led into his own house, a moderate amount of pumping on the part of everyone keeping the reservoir well filled.

Finally, a few of the inhabitants of the Valley, more keen than the rest, reflected that it was unnecessary to weary themselves with pumping, so long as everyone else kept at work. The Hill of Prosperity looked very attractive; and they therefore mounted to a convenient point, and put a large pipe into the reservoir, through which they drew off copious supplies of water without further trouble. The number of those who gave up pumping and withdrew to the Hill was at first so small that the loss did not add very much to the work of the mass of the people, who still kept to their pumping, and it did not occur to them to complain; but those who could followed the others up the Hill until it was all occupied, and by this time, although those who remained in the Valley did find their pumping a good deal harder than it was when all who used the water joined in the work, yet every one had become so accustomed to some people using the reservoir water without doing any pumping that it had come to be considered all right, and still there were no complaints. Meanwhile, the people on the Hill of Prosperity having nothing to do but enjoy the prospect, some of them began to explore the neighboring country, and soon discovered another valley at the foot of the Hill, running parallel with the Valley of Industry, and called the Valley of Idleness, and in it were a few people who had wandered from the former Valley (for the two were connected at the farther end), and who were living in abject misery, with no water, and apparently no means of getting any, so long as they stayed where they were. The people from the Hill of Prosperity were very much shocked at the suffering they found. "What a shame!" they cried. "The poor things have no water! We have plenty and to spare, so let us lead a pipe from the reservoir down into their Valley." No sooner said than done: the pipe was carried into the Valley of Idleness, and the people were made more comfortable. But as soon as the news was brought into the Valley of Industry, some of the pumpers who were tired or weak, and some who were only lazy, left their pumping, and hastened into the neighboring Valley, to enjoy the "free" water; but the pipe was not very large, and soon there was want and suffering again, and the people from Prosperity Hill were much disturbed, and decided to lay down another small pipe, which they did. But the result was the same, for the new supply of water attracted more people from the Valley of Industry. And so it went on, new pipe, more people, new pipe, more people, until the inhabitants of Prosperity Hill were full of distress about it, and exclaimed, "It seems a hopeless task to try to make these people happy and comfortable!" And they would have given up in despair, but a new idea occurred to them; and they said, "They do not seem to know how to take very good care of their children, and we will therefore take their children from them, and teach them to be comfortable and happy." So they built large, fine houses for the children, and they carried water in large pipes into the houses. And some of them said, "Let us put faucets, so as to teach them to turn on the water when they need it." But others said: "Oh, no! How troublesome it is to have to turn a faucet when you need water! Let them have it as we do, free." And sometimes one or other would suggest that, perhaps, after all, it was not quite right to waste so much of the water from the reservoir, and that the large pipe itself, which supplied the Hill of Prosperity, ought to have some means of checking the flow; but the answer was. "It is necessary and right that the water should be wasted; for otherwise the people in the Valley of Industry would have nothing to do, and they would starve." Usually, however, the Prosperity Hill people were too much engaged in taking care of the inhabitants of the Valley of Idleness to give much thought to those of the Valley of Industry; and their anxiety was quite magnified, for they had to keep up a perpetual watchfulness, the people increasing so fast that it was necessary constantly to lay more pipe to keep them from the most abject suffering, and even this device never succeeded for very long, as I have said.

In fact, no one thought much about the Valley of Industry or its people. Those in the Valley of Idleness only thought of them long enough to reflect how silly they were to keep on pumping all the time and making their backs and arms ache, when they might have water without any exertion, by simply moving into their Valley. The children born in the Valley of Idleness did not even know there was a Valley of Industry, or any pumps, or any pumpers, or a reservoir: they thought the water grew in pipes, and ran out because it was its nature to. As for the people of the Hill of

Prosperity, they were, as we have seen, rather confused in their views in this particular; and, besides thinking that their waste of the water from the reservoir was what kept the people in the Valley of Industry from starving, they used to also say sometimes: "How good it is for those people to have such nice, steady work to do! how strong it makes their back and arms! how it hardens their muscles! What a nice, independent set of people they are! and *what* a splendid opportunity of pure, life-giving water they get out of our reservoir!"

Meanwhile, you can imagine, though they could not, that it was rather hard on the men in the Valley of Industry, not only to have the water they pumped up drawn off at the top to supply two other communities, but also to have their own ranks thinned and their work increased by the loss of those who were tempted into the Valley of Idleness, to live on what the Prosperity Hill people and the Valley of Idleness people like to call euphemistically "free water," because they got it free, though actually it was not free at all; the Valley of Industry people paid for it with their blood and muscle.

I might go on to tell you how the situation was still further complicated and made harder for them, and indeed for almost everyone, when a few of them obtained control of the inexhaustible subterranean springs; but here, I think, the allegory may end for the purposes of this Conference, and it seems to me to teach a lesson which we may well heed.

Name _____

Date _____

1. What were the primary ideas contained in Lowell's allegory?

   _____

   _____

   _____

   _____

   _____

   _____

2. Does Lowell seem to see the problems of individuals as rooted in personal deficits, environmental deficits, or both? Explain.

   _____

   _____

   _____

   _____

   _____

   _____

3. Think about a specific legislative issue currently or recently debated at the state or local level—welfare reform or health care reform, for example. Given Lowell's views on relief, what values might she have expressed, and what views might she have taken on that issue?

   _____

   _____

   _____

   _____

_____

_____

_____

4. If Lowell were alive today, which of the policymakers and politicians in your state, or representing you in Congress, would she support? Why?

_____

_____

_____

_____

_____

_____

_____

5. Do you think that Lowell's sentiments would represent the mainstream of the profession as you understand it? Why or why not?

_____

_____

_____

_____

_____

_____

_____

WORKOUT 2   Learning From the Social Work Community

As you may have read in your social work textbook or heard in a lecture, the roots of the social work profession lie in the two decades leading up to the Progressive Era, beginning with the founding of the Charity Organization Society (in Buffalo, New York in 1877), and ending with the publication of *Social Diagnosis* (Richmond, 1917), the first textbook used in the first School of Social Work (at Columbia University). These two events have come to be seen as major milestones in the development of the "individual helping" stream of social work activity, which remains one of the primary models for social work practice today.

The opening of Hull House, the first settlement house, in Chicago in 1889 is widely viewed as the seminal event in the development of the second stream of social work activity: the social reform movement. This movement, characterized by a recognition of the influence of structural or environmental barriers to the realization of human potential, is recognizable today as "macrolevel" or social policy practice.

Both of these streams of practice, transfigured by time as well as social and economic exigencies, are what give social work its uniqueness within the pantheon of helping professions: (a) working with individuals to alleviate their distress and enable the fullest use of human potential and (b) advocating for social change by working to reduce those environmental barriers, often through social policy initiatives.

Our history is truly an illustrious one that generations of social workers have relished repeating to our newest professionals. Undoubtedly, your instructors will invoke the names, ideals, and writings of Addams, Richmond, and many others who have shaped the profession. However, remember that history is written continuously; thus future generations will read and reflect upon the words of current scholars and activists.

You can contribute to that history either by becoming a leader yourself or by chronicling the lives and times of those leaders who live in our midst now. It is the latter that is the focus of this workout.

Location

Outside class

Purpose

1. To increase skill in the discovery of living resource material in historical research.
2. To learn more about the development of the profession, or the social services in your community, from a historical perspective.
3. To learn how to develop a historical research question.
4. To exercise your skills of interviewing.

Background

The conduct of historical research using the informational interview of someone who was present during a time or event of interest to you can be an exciting endeavor. It allows you to ask questions and, when appropriate, examine documents in their possession about a period in which you are interested and to draw your own conclusions about its meaning. This makes *you* an expert on your subject rather than a biographer or historian who has already done the work for you.

Any research endeavor requires careful planning prior to execution, and the informational interview is no different. When conducting interviews with persons present at an event of historical significance, you need to read about the event, if possible, and have some questions prepared. If you have selected someone to interview whose ideas and ideals, you believe, shaped social services in your area in some way, gather background material related to the configuration of social services before that person came along, what some of the barriers to change were perceived by others to be, and the like.

You should also be prepared to have your assumptions challenged and myths debunked. For example, we lionize Jane Addams today because of her strong commitment to poverty amelioration and social change and her apparently feminist commitments regarding the role of women in public life. Yet Jane Addams did not believe in federal intervention in the care of the poor. That was one of the reasons why she was so committed to Hull House—it was privately funded. A limited federal government is an idea most often embraced by conservatives, but no one thinks of Addams as a conservative! So be prepared to come across the unexpected.

Directions

1. In consultation with your instructor, select a historical research question that you would like to answer, focusing on someone in your community. This may be done as a group project.

You want to interview a person who was influential in the development of social services, the ideas that shaped the development of the profession in your area, or a social worker who successfully organized for social change. This person might be any of the following:

- A retired professor from your school or department who may be able to speak on the establishment of the social work major within your college or university and might have also held some interesting and important positions in the field of social work prior to becoming an academician. You may wish to examine the professor's perceptions of social work now and then, or you may be interested in recording an oral history of how the social work major got started. You may also be interested in the sum total of such persons' contributions to and observations of social work over the many decades of their professional life. You will thus frame your interview accordingly.

- A local social worker, perhaps retired and living nearby, who was at the creation of one of the social service agencies presently operating in your community. This person may be willing to be interviewed about some of the controversies that surrounded the creation of the agency, the persons who first thought about starting it, and the like.

- A community organizer (preferably with a social work background) who organized constituent groups for social change. For example, is there a social worker who successfully lobbied, either locally or at the state level, for services to battered women before domestic violence was recognized as a problem? Or is there someone in your community who was active in a civil rights campaign (organizing African Americans in the South during the civil rights movement, organizing to press for the rights of persons with disabilities, organizing migrant workers, etc.)? Such persons had a unique vantage point from which to view the changes they fought for and may have some interesting notions about what remains to be done and what the struggles of tomorrow are likely to be.

2. Where appropriate, you may also wish to avail yourself of archival material housed in a local agency (including the agency's first by-laws, minutes from meetings, correspondence from funding sources, etc.) that would shed additional light on your topic.

3. You may wish to begin the research process by writing a formal letter to the person(s) you would like to interview and following up with a phone call. Prior to the interview, you may wish to read some background material. Once you have done that, prepare a list of questions you would like to have answered, but always be ready, once in the interview, to follow the respondent and ask follow-up questions.

4. Using a tape recorder to supplement your own notes, conduct the interview.

5. Upon completion of your data collection procedure, write a report of your efforts in the Workout 2 Workspace, answering the questions contained therein.

WORKOUT 2 *Workspace*

Name _____

Date _____

1. What question(s) did you wish your respondent (interviewee) to answer?

_____

_____

_____

_____

_____

2. What sources, if any, did you use (besides the respondent) both to prepare you to make the most of your interview and to help you answer your question?

_____

_____

_____

_____

_____

3. What degree of difficulty (not at all, moderate, or very difficult) would you assign to this project in terms of (a) finding a suitable respondent and (b) finding appropriate background material to help prepare you for the interview? Why?

_____

_____

_____

_____

_____

4. What did you learn from this project about your particular research question?

_____

_____

_____ —

_____

_____

_____

5. What surprised you the most?

_____

_____

_____

_____

_____

_____

6. Additional comments:

_____

_____

_____

_____

_____

WORKOUT 3 Debating Contemporary Issues in Social Welfare

One of the most critical skills a social worker can possess is the ability to shape public opinion, perhaps the most influential force in daily living. Public opinion represents the global judgment of some critical mass of citizens on an issue of public concern. All public issues are inherently conflictual; it is the responsibility of community leaders to listen to the diversity of voices and then to resolve the conflict (Windes & Hastings, 1965).

All citizens have a vested interest in the manner in which public issues are resolved. Social workers, however, with their firsthand knowledge of the impact of public issues on the private lives of clients, have not only a vested interest but an ethical obligation to their clients to influence public opinion in a way that will expand choices or resources for them.

Given the inherently conflictual nature of public issue resolution, the most common way in which such matters are resolved is through an adversarial process of argumentation or debate. This process requires that we be able to analyze controversial issues and formulate propositions that reveal those issues. It also requires that we then use those skills to prove our conclusions to others in society, hoping ultimately to resolve the controversy in our clients' or our own favor.

For many people, the prospect of argument is not an appealing one. A distaste for conflict, an aversion to public speaking, or sometimes a lack of confidence in the position we have taken makes us reticent about assuming a vigorous advocacy role. However, it is important to remember that part of the social worker's job is to help empower or enable marginalized citizens to act on their own behalf. If we are unable or unwilling to exude confidence about ourselves and our abilities, we are highly unlikely to inspire others by our example.

If you are naturally drawn to the profession of social work, it is likely because you have strong opinions about some of the policies that govern the lives of clients and have some ideas about the way you would like to see things change. This is as it should be. The purpose of this workout is to help you become the most forceful advocate you can be by giving you practice in the skills required to persuade others to adopt your position on a public policy of interest to you.

Location

In/outside class combination

Purpose

1. To practice and sharpen critical thinking and persuasion skills.
2. To learn more about a controversial policy issue of importance to you.
3. To begin to get a feel for the work of an advocate—an important social work role.

Background

During the course of one's professional life, the social worker is called upon to fulfill many roles—broker, resource manager, mediator, and counselor, among others. An equally challenging role is that of advocate, one who uses especially the skills of motivation, strategy development, and persuasion to influence policies in ways that are favorable to clients.

Although this role is central to social work, the skills of the advocate are not well developed in most social workers (Hoffman & Sallee, 1994). This, in part, may be the reason why so few social workers feel comfortable in this role. Yet it is in this role that the most hallowed professionals in our history—Jane Addams, Florence Kelley, Bertha Reynolds, and others—made their indelible marks.

Whether you are testifying before a legislative committee, campaigning for a cause or a candidate, developing winning strategies, or working with the media, the heart of the work is persuading others that your position is the correct one. This is done by thoroughly understanding all the arguments both against and in favor of your position (which also means being able to anticipate them) and the facts and opinions of the audience you are trying to persuade.

It is hoped that upon completion of this workout you will feel comfortable, even confident, that given the opportunity you will be able to contribute to an advocacy effort in your community.

Directions

1. The class should be divided into groups of four to eight, depending on class size. About six to seven groups should be formed.
2. Each group should divide itself in half, with one side considered the "affirmative" team and the other side the "rebuttal" team.

3. Each team should select a captain. These captains are responsible for negotiating the selection of a topic (either from the group listed below or one of their own choosing, with the consent of the instructor).

Some topics you may wish to consider are these:

- Resolved: that persons with terminal diseases and experiencing pain who wish to end their lives with the assistance of a physician should be able to do so.

- Resolved: that minors facing unwanted pregnancy obtain the consent of parent(s) or guardian(s) before obtaining an abortion.

- Resolved: that persons receiving TANF (formerly AFDC) be allowed no more than 60 months of benefit payments over a lifetime.

- Resolved: that a parent reported to child welfare authorities by a child for possible abuse and neglect of his/her children be allowed to face the accuser in a court of law.

- Resolved: that authorities notify communities to which a sexual offender is returning upon his or her release from prison or a halfway house.

- Resolved: that race of an applicant be a consideration in the admissions processes of colleges and universities.

- Resolved: that Social Security revert from an entitlement program to a means-tested program (in which the income and assets of the Social Security applicant are taken into consideration).

4. Once the topic has been selected, teams should get to work on the development of their arguments. *Ample time should be given to this task—about 1 to 2 weeks.*

5. The "affirmative" team is charged with constructing the arguments in favor of the issue; the "rebuttal" team's job is to anticipate as many of those arguments as possible and to pose questions to the affirmative team that expose the fallacies in those arguments after the affirmative team has presented its case. It is then the rebuttal team's job to present arguments against the policy, which the affirmative team is then to question. The actual process should take about 30-45 minutes; each side should assume that it will have about 20 minutes both to present its argument and answer questions. Two people from each team can present their arguments, with another two answering the questions from the opposing side. All team members are to take part in constructing arguments, anticipating the questions from the other side (and the answers thereto), and developing strategies for winning.

6. Each debate is presented to the class, after which the instructor may wish to engage the class in a discussion about which side prevailed, and why (it is not always the side you agree with!). A scoring sheet for the debates such as the one at the back of this workout may also be used. Teams and their representatives should be judged upon their ability to analyze the issue, present their reasoning, provide evidence for their position, organize their argument coherently, and effectively refute their opponent.

WORKOUT 3 *Workspace*

Name _____

Date _____

1. My debate team is taking the (affirmative/rebuttal) position and consists of the following members:

   _____

   _____

   _____

   _____

   _____

   _____

   _____

2. Those charged with presenting our case are:

   _____ (Captain)

   _____ (will answer questions)

3. Our issue is:

   Resolved: _____

   _____

   _____

   _____

   _____

   _____

   _____

Notetaking Space:

Issues to include in our argument (and supporting evidence):

_____

_____

_____

_____

Questions to anticipate and responses:

_____

_____

_____

_____

_____

Final Draft of Argument

_____

_____

_____

_____

_____

_____

_____

_____

_____

_____

Scoring Sheet for Judges

(This sheet may be copied to score each debate.)

Topic: _____

Date: _____ Judge: _____

Rank the speakers in this debate from 1 to 4, with 1 being best.

Then, rate the effectiveness of their arguments on a scale of 1 to 10, with 10 being best.

	Debater	*Rank*	*Team*	*Effectiveness Rating*
Affirmative	_____	_____	_____	_____
Q and A	_____	_____	_____	_____
Rebuttal	_____	_____	_____	_____
Q and A	_____	_____	_____	_____

Comments and reasons for decisions:

_____

_____

_____

_____

_____

_____

_____

_____

_____

_____

_____

_____

WORKOUT 4 Budgeting a Poverty-Level Income

As this introduction is being written, two interrelated dialogues are taking place in our nation's capital. The first one, about welfare reform, centers on the question of how best to move people who are on welfare—a term that usually refers to the Transitional Assistance to Needy Families (TANF) program (formerly AFDC), whose beneficiaries are mostly women and their young children)—from **dependence** to **self-sufficiency**, the latter of which is usually defined by politicians of all stripes as a lack of need for governmental income supports. The second dialogue, narrower and more likely to be quickly resolved, focuses on the minimum wage and the question of whether it should be raised, over some period of time, to a level closer to the **poverty line**.

What is the poverty line? This is an important question, with implications for both of the policy debates noted above. Briefly, the term is used to define the uppermost income threshold for families defined as being "in poverty." Although many have argued that the federal government should use a "relative approach" in defining poverty (i.e., base our definition on a standard of living relative to that of other community members; Rodgers, 1984, calls this *relative deprivation*), in general, the federal government has chosen to use an "absolute approach" in which an assumption is made that a certain level of income is required to purchase a minimum of goods and services necessary to an individual's or family's welfare. Those with an income level below that minimum are considered "in poverty."

Many social work and social welfare policy textbooks discuss in considerable detail the history and methods by which the Census Bureau arrives at poverty-level income threshold figures for families of varying sizes; this is a very complex discussion and beyond the purview of this workbook. Suffice it to say that the government's methods are based on patterns of family expenditures that are over three decades old.

There are two primary reasons why it is important for students of social welfare to understand the centrality of the poverty-line concept to their work as professionals. First, many clients are eligible for and rely on income support programs because they meet guidelines set by the state, which are influenced by the federal poverty-line calculation. The second reason is that just about every empirical examination of our national prosperity uses the poverty-line calculation as a critical measure. When scholars talk about "the growth of poverty" in this country or, more obliquely, "the downward spiral of many working-class families into poverty," they are talking about the poverty-line calculation, which controls for family size.

As of 1997, the poverty level for a two-parent family of four is a bit over $16,000. Two parents, both working at the current minimum-wage level full-time and for 50 weeks per year, earn a gross income of $17,000. Thus, this family is considered "low income" but not "in poverty."

What do you think is the minimum income necessary to raise a family? Is it possible to purchase the minimum in goods and services necessary with a joint income of $17,000? Maybe you grew up in a low-income household or are close to others who grew up in poverty. If that is so, you are in an excellent position to assist your classmates in this workout because these are the questions to be addressed.

WORKOUT 4 *Instructions*

Where

In and outside class

Purpose

1. To enable you to think critically about what it means to live "in poverty."
2. To enable you to assess realistically where you think the poverty threshold should be.
3. To gain some insights into the assumptions that have informed the debates about the "minimum wage" and welfare reform.

Background

In our dual roles as citizens and as serious students of social work, we need to become informed about changes proposed by our federal and state governments which are likely to affect our clients. Similarly, we need to carefully examine the facts and assumptions on which competing arguments are built, moving beyond rhetoric to serious examination.

During the Reagan presidency, Agriculture Secretary John Block wanted to demonstrate to the American people the adequacy of the standard "economy diet plan," developed for a family of four by the Department of Agriculture. To that end, he put his household of four on the economy diet. For a week, the family lived within the dietary guidelines, spending the allowable food allotment to buy their food. At the end of the week, the Secretary pronounced his experiment a success, having managed successfully to feed the household for a week on what many thought was an inadequate amount of money for the family.

Assuming that the Secretary did as he said, there are a few problems with his "experiment." First, a household of healthy individuals, in an extremely time-limited period, is not going to suffer significant ill effects (such as stunted physical, mental, and social development in children and chronic disorders, such as diabetes, in adults) from an inadequate diet. Persons who live at or below the poverty line may be subsisting on such diets indefinitely. Second, the psychological advantage the Block family had, knowing that their "deprivation" was very time-limited and controlled, is an advantage not available to those whose situation he was trying to emulate.

Mr. Block thus proved very little with his experiment. However, he is to be commended for trying, if only in a limited way, to experience the conditions of those affected by his department's policies. This workout has been developed to create the facilitating conditions for thinking about the real difficulties of living at the economic margins.

A cautionary note, though: As difficult to think about as this may be, it is no substitute for actually living that life.

Directions

1. Your instructor will divide your class into small groups of four to seven people. Once this has been done, turn to the workspace and peruse each section of the budget. Chances are that you really do not know what constitutes a reasonable expenditure for many of these items—for example, if you live in an apartment where all utilities are paid by the landlord, or if you do not pay for health insurance, you may not know what these things would reasonably cost. Thus, your first task is to divide up these groups of expenditures and assign two or three to each member of your group—for example, one person could take housing, utilities, and maintenance; another could take education, insurance, and food; and so on.

2. Members should then take one week to conduct some research to determine what might constitute a reasonable expense for the items in the expenditure groups to which they were assigned. For example, if you were assigned **Housing,** what would a reasonable home mortgage payment be for a small, two-bedroom house? Or, if you chose for the family to live in a rental unit, how much is rent in your community for an inexpensive apartment? If they own their home, do they have mortgage insurance? How much is that typically? Renter's insurance? If you were assigned **Food** as an expenditure group, what is a reasonable estimate of grocery costs for a family of four for a month? Should there be any money for eating out?

3. Once each person has conducted research on the assigned sections, turn to the Workspace section and develop the rest of the budget for the family, broadly described below, which allows them the minimum monthly income necessary for their welfare. Fill in each line item under the right-hand column, labeled "My Estimate" (if you see a line item that you think is an unnecessary expense, leave that item blank).

4. Now you are ready to reconvene with your group. At this point, everyone should have completed some research into specific areas and have some general sense of what they think are reasonable expenses in the other areas. The group's job now is to reach some consensus about each expense. For example, is it possible for this family to own their own home in your community (or even desirable), or should they rent? Is any money allotted to meals out and, if not, does everyone agree that never eating out is a reasonable expectation? Whatever the final figure that your group comes up with for each item, that figure must represent a consensus of the group's view. Each of you should note in your Workspace the dollar figure that the group agrees on for each item (in the left-hand column), as well as the dollar figures you originally thought were reasonable (right-hand column). If any expenses are met through nonconventional means (bartering is an example), this should be noted in your Workspace.

5. Once all groups have completed their calculations, the class reconvenes and your instructor guides the discussion. To prepare, think about the following questions:

   a. Prior to beginning the workout, did you believe that the government poverty-line calculation for a family of four represented a reasonable estimate of the funds needed for a particular family?

   b. Did you overestimate, underestimate, or fairly accurately estimate the funds needed for this family prior to this workout?

   c. What are some of the budget items you consider necessary but had not really thought about prior to this workout?

   d. What are some of the budget items you consider unnecessary?

   e. Has this workout changed any of your thinking about how poverty is defined, or how one defines what is essential for an adequate standard of living?

WORKOUT 5 Influencing Local Public Policy

One of the previous workouts in this book (#3) emphasized the importance of the social work role of advocacy, or working to make laws and environmental conditions more favorable to clients. It was noted in that workout that your abilities to advance a cogent argument and successfully anticipate and rebut the arguments of the other side are crucial advocacy skills. Equally important, however, is an understanding of the many avenues open for influencing policy available to interested private citizens. It is the premise of this workbook that some number of you will not become social workers and thus have no clients to advocate for. We hope, however, that you will always be vitally interested in the affairs of your local community and willing to lend your talents and skills to a good cause.

In every community large and small, public policy issues arise that capture the hearts and minds of its citizens. In the small college town where I live, for example, there are a number of ongoing controversies that have wrought extreme disagreement from disparate groups of citizens. The most recent revolves around the decision by the School Board to close three neighborhood public schools. Board members believe that their fiduciary responsibility to the taxpaying public requires them to close schools when they become too costly to run. All three schools have low enrollment and/or structural problems requiring repair. Thus, the cost per pupil is, in the opinion of the Board, prohibitive. However, neighborhood families and others in the community disagree. They note that these schools serve low-income families who rely on a neighborhood school that is relatively close to home. Almost all the parents work, making transporting the children by car to the next closest school very difficult. Riding the bus would make the day prohibitively long for the children (many would have rides of over an hour each coming and going). Furthermore, the quality of their education would suffer in a large school with less favorable teacher-pupil ratios. In other words, the controversy seems to boil down to cost-benefit versus quality of life, a common theme in local public controversies.

Another issue in my community (for many years now) has to do with the desire of the County Commissioners to build a trafficway by which people coming in from the "bedroom communities" further west can access the center of town more quickly. The most obvious (and least costly) way to accomplish this, however, requires that the road be built through a tract of wetlands, a fragile and relatively rare ecosystem that environmentalists argue is crucial to the maintenance of a variety of species of plants and other living things. Equally important, the Native American community argues that this ground is hallowed and has long been a place of prayer and spiritual solace. To build a road through such ground, then, will disrupt a delicate ecosystem and diminish spiritual practice for a group of citizens.

Undoubtedly, your community is in the midst of similar controversies. Perhaps it has to do with public transportation or funding for local social services. Maybe your college or university is currently focusing on an issue of importance to you, such as changing admissions requirements, raising fees, or closing a department.

I am confident that, regardless of where you are, public policy issues of importance to you are being discussed in the newspapers, in editorials, on television, in neighborhood meetings, and the like. Chances are that, while you have a stake in the outcome, you have not become involved. This workout provides that opportunity.

WORKOUT 5 *Instructions*

Location

In class or E-mail

Purpose

1. To provide you with an opportunity to lend your voice to the resolution of a local public policy issue.
2. To socialize you to the process of participating in civic dialogue.
3. To help you clarify your thinking on a local issue of importance to your community or university.

Background

Community participation can take several forms. If you feel that there are issues being discussed that are important but that you do not have sufficient information about to form an opinion, the first step is to educate yourself. You can do this by reading the papers, talking to local officials (who do their very best to communicate with potential voters), attending public forums on the issue, and, where relevant, conducting library research. Just learning about an issue can constitute participation. However, once you have come to some conclusions about where you stand, it is time for you to enter the dialogical fray.

A common misconception about community participation is that one person cannot possibly make much difference. In my own life, I have seen the power of one person speaking or writing eloquently and with conviction about issues of great importance to that person, change either the terms of the dialogue or the opinions of the policymakers. Conversely, the person who speaks forcefully but inarticulately or who advances *ad hominem* attacks against the opposing side can do irreparable damage to the cause that person advocates.

This workout requires you to write a letter supporting or opposing an issue currently under consideration in your community or at your university. Although it is appropriate to write and send letters to municipal officials, this letter should be written for your local newspaper so that it reaches as wide an audience as possible (keep in mind that this is an assignment, unless you want to, you need not actually send it to the newspaper). Successful completion of this task requires that you know as much as possible about your issue, so you may wish to talk to knowledgeable people or peruse the newspaper in advance of this assignment to learn as much as you can.

Now is the time to start making a difference!

Directions

1. Select a public issue currently under debate in your community. This may be an issue concerning the funding of social services or a "quality of life" issue (e.g., proposals for housing the homeless in the community,

keeping at-risk youths out of trouble, revising Affirmative Action policies, or expanding public transportation). You may select an issue of interest to constituent groups at your college or university as well, such as changing admission requirements, increased tuition or activity fees, and the like.

2. If you are uncertain of the appropriateness of your issue for this assignment, check with your instructor.

3. Once your topic is established, be prepared to write a draft of a letter to the editor of your local newspaper stating your position and using information you have collected from others to back it up (e.g., others interested in this issue, news articles, other research if necessary). This letter will either be written in class or on computer outside the class, depending on the direction of your instructor. You may use whatever information you have that will best advance your cause, including solid factual information or moral arguments. Should you choose the latter, however, it is best for the purposes of this assignment to refrain from making your issue a religious one.

4. Once you have completed your draft, exchange your letter with the student sitting behind you or next to you if the assignment is done in class or do so via E-mail with another student. This person should provide you with feedback on your letter, using the questions supplied in the Workspace. Once that task is completed, your letter will be returned.

5. Respond to the feedback by either correcting your letter along the dimensions suggested, or defending, in the space provided, why you have decided to stick with your original text.

All workspace sheets should be turned in to your instructor at the end of the allotted time. (If you completed your assignment using email, please attach your draft, the response of the student with whom you exchanged letters, your response to his/her feedback, and your final draft letter.)

WORKOUT 5 *Workspace*

Name _____

Date _____

Date:

Address:

Dear _____:

_____

_____

_____

_____

_____

_____

_____

_____

_____

_____

_____

_____

_____

Sincerely,

(Your Signature)

Peer Feedback:

1. Did the writer present a compelling argument (or set of arguments) for his/her point of view? Explain.

_____

_____

_____

_____

_____

2. In what ways, if any, might the writer have expressed his/her views more effectively?

_____

_____

_____

_____

Letter Writer's Response to Evaluator: (a full, corrected text of the letter is to be turned in to your instructor)

_____

_____

_____

_____

_____

_____

_____

_____

_____

2 THE SOCIAL WORK PROFESSION

WORKOUT 6 Understanding Social Work Regulation in Your State

At the present time, some regulation of the profession of social work exists in every state in the United States. Usually, this regulation takes the form of a system of licensure. *Licensure* is officially defined as

> a process by which an agency of government grants permission to an individual to engage in a given occupation, upon finding that the applicant has attained the minimal degree of competency required to ensure that the public health, safety, and welfare will be reasonably well protected. (Karls, 1992, p. 53)

In other words, having a system in place that requires social workers to meet minimal standards for practice ostensibly ensures the protection of the service consumer from incompetent practitioners. Licensing also clarifies the "scope of practice," that is, what the social worker may lawfully do. For example, in Kansas, the social worker may diagnose mental disorders (this is included in "scope of practice" statements that govern what professional social workers can do) but in no state can the social worker prescribe medication (not included in "scope of practice.").

Given the pervasiveness of licensure in this country, it seems clear that such regulation is viewed as desirable. Both the profession and the public generally believe in the concept. However, not everyone agrees that the regulation of the profession is a good thing. Mathis (1992), for example, believes that licensing has a pernicious effect:

> [It] narrows the scope and the nature of services delivered to people of color, . . . restricts job opportunities for [minorities] . . . by utilizing invalid and biased testing and formal, university-based education as the basic screening mechanisms for entering the profession, and screens out disproportionately . . . non-mainstream perspectives. (p. 59)

In other words, the institution of licensing is inherently racist and serves to maintain race- and class-based inequalities.

If the purpose of licensing is to protect the public from incompetence, you ought to know what its converse—competence—is. Regulation, coupled with the absence of such a definition, invites the criticism of "overregulation." Here is an example: Recently, Kansas compelled a teenager to cease and desist the practice of cosmetology without a license. The nature of her crime? She was earning money (albeit less than a licensed beautician) by braiding the hair of friends and acquaintances into "cornrows," tiny braids all over the head that take a very long time to do. When a group of licensed, professional beauticians heard about the girl and her business, they brought her to the attention of the local authorities. Citizens in the community, irritated that the young girl was being punished, in effect, for showing some entrepreneurial instinct, questioned the decision to shut her down. Local beauticians defended the decision, stating that they had gone to beauty school, had learned about the skeletal structure of the head and about many different kinds of hair preparations, and that practices such as this girl's were dangerous to the public. What do you think? Did the cease-and-desist order protect the public? Or did the system of licensing simply keep a competent person from exercising her ability to compete in the marketplace?

This is not a small matter, either in theory or in practice, for the terms of the argument speak directly to the ongoing conflict within the profession about how it can remain true to its historical, anti-elitist mission while striving for the trappings of elitism—high pay and high status—that licensing requirements may reflect.

For some of you, licensing issues will become salient before you graduate, because your state regulates entry-level practice. Others of you will not need to consider licensure unless or until you attain a graduate degree. The question of the levels at which your state licenses can best be answered by your instructor. Nevertheless, it is important to understand the terms and conditions of attaining a license and keeping it active in the state in which you intend to practice, as well as getting a general sense of the whole regulation enterprise.

WORKOUT 6 *Instructions*

Location

In and outside class

Purpose

1. To understand the professional social work regulatory system in your state.
2. To learn more about how social work regulates itself across the country.
3. To gain the knowledge and understanding necessary for developing a critical perspective on the issue of licensure.

Background

This workout is based on the presumption that you have decided to attain an education that will get you to your goal of being a social worker. When we make the decision about what occupation or profession to pursue, we rarely think about what is required beyond the formal education component.

Graduation, however, is usually but one (albeit usually the most difficult) step toward being sanctioned by the state to practice your profession.

Persons contemplating entering the social work profession would be well served by learning about licensure requirements in their state, as well as answers to many other questions. For example, some states have licensing **reciprocity** with other states, which means that if you meet the requirements for licensing in one state, then the other state accepts your qualifications. Does your state have reciprocity? Another question often asked has to do with whether or not a student who has committed certain crimes in the past can be summarily prevented from being licensed by the state. How does your state handle an applicant's criminal record?

More important, though, what you learn about licensing will help you develop your own perspective about the functions it serves in society. That is the primary purpose of this workout.

Directions

1. Your instructor invites to class the credentialing specialist for your State Board to discuss licensing issues in your state. You should prepare for this talk by developing a list of questions you would like answered. These questions should relate to the specific requirements for attaining a license at the various levels, the costs associated with attaining and maintaining a license, and whether exceptions or waivers are ever granted for either of those two things. You might also ask about the scope of practice. In other words, what does having a license actually allow you to do? Query the credentialing specialist about reciprocity: Does your state have agreements with other states? On what grounds may a person be considered to be practicing social work without a

license? What happens to social workers who behave unethically? What other helping professionals are licensed through this same State Board? Are their requirements more, or less, stringent than those for social work? Take notes as part of this workout.

2. Your instructor then assigns each person in the class a state licensing board to write to, asking for specific information and answers to relevant questions. This part of the assignment can also be done in groups and takes almost no time. For example, one person in your group finds out the location of the State Board you have been assigned to write to (the Social Work Examination Service web page has links to addresses of all State Boards: **http://www.tiac.net/users/swes**). Another in your group writes the letter, asking that information be sent to the third member, who then is responsible for sharing that information.

3. On a day appointed by your instructor, all groups share the information they have gathered. Based on that information, your instructor leads you in a discussion about licensing and what you have learned.

WORKOUT 6 *Workspace*

Name _____

Date _____

Notes From Guest Speaker

_____

_____

_____

_____

_____

_____

_____

_____

_____

_____

_____

_____

_____

_____

_____

_____

_____

_____

_____

_____

_____

Use this page to note the specifics of the letter you sent to the State Board assigned you by your teacher.

Address of Board: _____

Information requested:

_____

_____

_____

_____

_____

Date the letter was mailed: _____

Person to whom information is to be sent: _____

Address: _____

_____

Notes to Remember From Class Discussion About Licensure Around the Country

_____

_____

_____

_____

_____

_____

_____

_____

_____

_____

1. Based on what you have learned about licensure, what is your perspective?

_____

_____

_____

_____

_____

_____

2. Do you think the requirements set forth actually protect the public from the incompetent?

_____

_____

_____

_____

_____

_____

3. Do states make any exceptions to accommodate persons for whom licensing poses barriers to the ability to earn a living?

_____

_____

_____

_____

_____

_____

_____

4. If not, do you think that such exceptions should be made, and if so, under what circumstances?

_____

_____

_____

_____

_____

5. Should anyone who meets the minimum requirements be granted a license?

_____

_____

_____

_____

_____

6. Are the sanctions for unethical behavior clear?

_____

_____

_____

_____

_____

7. What should the future of licensing be?

_____

_____

_____

_____

_____

WORKOUT 7 Using the Internet to Enhance Professional Socialization

A little over two decades ago, an article in *Social Work* heralded the beginning of the computer age in the social work profession (Hoshino & McDonald, 1975). Since then, the use of computers in social work has grown exponentially, as it has in every other professional field.

If you think about it, the means by which you have accessed information—to write papers, to apply for college loans, for the purchase of goods and services—has changed dramatically since you were in high school, even if you graduated only 2 or 3 years ago. Similarly, the information available to you about social work has virtually exploded, and the computer, and more specifically the Internet, of which the World Wide Web (or Web) is a major part, has been the driving force.

It would be impossible to detail for you all the resources available via the Internet (for a full explication of Internet applications for social workers, see Rivard, 1997). Furthermore, those of you with home computers and a modem are probably already familiar with many of those resources. However, even if you do not have a home computer, your university library and probably also your community library have access to the World Wide Web.

Recently, I spent a morning on the Web searching for resources for my own students. Like many of them, I have no natural affinity for computers, and like many academics, I seem to gravitate more to the rarefied spaces of the library stacks, where I can pick up a book and read words on paper. Nevertheless, neither my colleagues nor I can deny the incredible power of the information available to us only through this means.

Here is only a partial list of resources available through the Web that could prove invaluable for you:

- Opportunities to communicate with other social work students and working professionals around the country and the world
- Information about how to answer a classified ad, search effectively for a job, learn more about salaries
- Web pages for many schools of social work in both the United States and Europe, with links to important information on their admissions policies, philosophical orientation, field placements, schedules, what their alumni are doing, and so on
- Special interest news and discussion groups on an incredibly wide variety of topics, such as child abuse, alcoholism, domestic violence, disability, mental illness, feminism, sprirtuality, ethics, and so forth
- Web pages created by individual social workers who may wish to publicize their expertise in a particular area of practice, are looking for other jobs, or wish simply to communicate with like-minded individuals on a variety of topics
- Information/Web pages for advocacy groups and social policy initiatives that you may wish to become involved with

The exciting part of this new technology is that you can access information on just about anything you are curious about, instantaneously. Thus, as a beginning social worker learning new ideas in school and curious about what others in the profession think of these ideas, you are in a position to make discoveries in a way that previous generations of students could not.

WORKOUT 7 *Instructions*

Location

Outside class

Purpose

1. To increase your general ability to use the Internet effectively.
2. To provide you with a hands-on experience in accessing resources relevant to the beginning social worker.
3. To enhance your socialization to the profession by enabling you to become acquainted with the people, places, values, and issues important to its members.

Background

Understanding the potential of the Internet and knowing how to access its resources is an indispensable skill, regardless of where you live, your career aspirations, or anything else. As a professional social worker, you will one day encounter a client problem for which neither you nor your agency colleagues have the answer. Imagine then being able to pose your problem to an infinitely large group of colleagues in cyberspace, who have the capacity to respond immediately. Bound by a uniform value base but trained in a variety of different perspectives, these colleagues can enhance your practice tremendously, just as you can theirs.

Directions

1. For this exercise, you obviously need access to a computer with a World Wide Web browser, such as Netscape or Internet Explorer. If you do not have your own computer, your university and/or community library may.

   Due to limited resources, you may need to reserve computer time in the libraries. Furthermore, if you have had either very limited or no experience working with the Internet, you may wish to make an appointment with the librarian.

2. Now you are ready to proceed, following the steps in the Workspace. Staple your computer-printed work your Workspace page when you turn it in.

WORKOUT 7 *Workspace*

Name _____

Date _____

1. To conduct a search of the World Wide Web, you will need a "search engine." Click on "Net Search" to see the search engine(s) available to you. What are they?

   _____   _____   _____

   _____   _____   _____

   _____   _____   _____

2. Go to the search engine called Yahoo (although you can reach Yahoo just by clicking your mouse on the word, "Yahoo," a better way for the purposes of this workout is to change the URL [for "uniform resource locator," better known as just the "Web address"] to http://www.Yahoo.com). Once you have done that, click on "social science," which is one of the listed subheadings. After you have done that, click on "social work," a sub-subheading under "social science." What shows up at this site?

   _____

   _____

   _____

   _____

3. These subject areas are written in what is called "hypertext." This means that clicking on these words with your mouse will link you to other sites. Explore all of these sites in "social work," beginning with the first one, by clicking on the hypertexted words of interest to you at each of the sites you encounter. Discuss below where this exploration led you and what you learned about resources available to you.

   _____

   _____

   _____

   _____

   _____

4. Now change the search engine to Infoseek. You can do this by clicking on "Net Search" or "Net Directory" on the panel at the top of your screen and then on the word "Infoseek." Once you have done this, you are ready to conduct a search within your particular area of interest. Since Infoseek "reads" quotation marks and the addition sign, it is important to use them for the words, phrases, or areas of interest. Thus, if you are interested in social work practice with persons with serious mental illness, type into the search box the words "social work" + "serious mental illness." You could also narrow your search by using more search terms, or more words within the quotation marks. An example of this might be "social work practice" + "serious mental illness" + "schizophrenia." Go ahead and try it. What terms did you type in?

_____

_____

_____

_____

How many "hits," or potentially interesting sites, were yielded?

_____

_____

_____

_____

5. Explore at least three of the sites that look the most interesting (you can certainly explore more beyond these three). What are some of the contemporary problems and issues in your area that have captured the attention of the profession, as evidenced by the information you found? Print out the first page from each of these three sites and turn them in with this assignment.

_____

_____

_____

_____

_____

_____

6. Having now conducted searches using two different search engines, which one was more fruitful in terms of information that you can use?

_____

_____

_____

_____

_____

_____

7. Many of the Web sites you came across were probably of questionable veracity. In other words, the information contained within some sites may have been opinion masquerading as fact, or information that is out of date or otherwise discredited. How should you, as a consumer of information using this technology, evaluate the relevance or tuth of the information, or the rigorousness of the research presented?

_____

_____

_____

_____

_____

_____

_____

_____

_____

_____

_____

_____

_____

_____

8. If the School of Social Welfare at your college or university has its own URL, go to that site now (if social work is a department within a larger college, such as liberal arts, or arts and sciences, or "anthropology, sociology, and social work," for example, you may need to start with that and then proceed to social work). Explore this site. What links does your school or department's page contain? What kind of information is contained therein that reflects your school's uniqueness?

_____

_____

_____

_____

_____

_____

9. Finally, project yourself into the future and pretend you are now a social worker with clients. How might the Internet help them as they seek to solve their problems?

_____

_____

_____

_____

_____

_____

WORKOUT 8   Shaping Public Perception of Social Work

If you are having difficulty making a choice about a major, you are certainly not alone. Those of us who made the decision to enter the social work profession did so, in many cases, after considering other "people-oriented" career paths. In the end, many of us chose social work because we believed it offered us a way to be helpful to people within a value framework that was consistent with our own. But many of us are also mindful that, for reasons both within and beyond our control, the public at large harbors perceptions of the profession that simply do not square with our experience. Here are some of the things I have heard from relatives, friends, and acquaintances when the topic of my profession comes up:

- All social workers are liberals (some think this is a good thing, others bad, but they all think it!).
- Social workers fail to take babies who are being abused or neglected out of the home.
- Social workers remove children who are NOT being abused or neglected from their homes, often on flimsy evidence.
- Social workers do the same things a psychiatrist does, only with less education.
- Social workers who do private practice make lots of money.
- Everyone who works in public social services is a social worker (in fact, even the majority of those working in public child welfare do not possess a social work degree).

If you choose social work as a career, you too will most likely hear things about social work that are inconsistent with your experience of the profession. It will be your responsibility, as a member, to correct falsehoods or offer alternative perceptions.

There are several ways that you can do this. One very easy way, is to CALL YOURSELF A SOCIAL WORKER! Not a family therapist, or a counselor, or an administrator. A big part of the problem has to do with our tendency to use job titles, which sometimes obscure our professional background.

Another way is to recognize the source of the misperception being promulgated and to address that. Since people are likely to develop their ideas based on what they see on television or read in the paper, those are good places to start. That is the central focus of this workout.

Location

Outside class; results reported in class

Purpose

1. To better understand the popular perception(s) of the social work profession and the means by which that perception is created.
2. To provide an opportunity for learning useful information-retrieval skills.
3. To provide a basis for discussing how you, as a beginning social worker or knowledgeable outsider, can contribute to an accurate perception of this profession.

Background

Recently I was home on a Friday night, channel surfing to my heart's content. Inadvertently, I came across a new television program (now off the air) about a crisis counseling and hotline center. Curious, I continued watching. When the actress portraying the center's director informed a client's parent that she had a master's degree in social work, I was hooked. This actress was young, beautiful, and appeared to be multiethnic. She was in a position of great responsibility, and while even I admit that we social workers do have our share of bad-hair days, she seemed incapable of waking up to one.

In truth, the plot was not realistic, based on my experience (to be fair, I have heard many lawyers complain that their jobs do not resemble TV lawyers', either), but it was entertaining, it focused on a real issue that many grapple with, and, most important, the social worker did not fit the stereotype of a tired, embittered bureaucrat. It suddenly occurred to me that, in reality, many people will never come in contact with a social worker and that the only impressions they have of us are from TV and newspapers.

Are you aware of the messages about social work conveyed by the media? You will be after completing this workout.

Directions

1. This portion of the workout requires you to use a general periodical database. A full-text, general news database, such as the Expanded Academic Index, InfoTrak, or, where available, Lexis-Nexis, would be excellent for the purposes of this assignment. Many students do not know about these databases; however, most libraries do have access to one or more of these, and they are invaluable sources of information for purposes both within and beyond academia. Given this lack of familiarity, I recommend that the newspaper portion of the assignment be done in groups of two to four. Groups should make appointments with the reference librarian to learn how to access the appropriate information.

2. Once you have accessed the general news database available at your school, search for current articles (start with the current year) in which the words "social work" or "social worker" have been used seven times in the article (any article that mentions these words less than seven times either is not really about social work or is an obituary about a social worker. You want neither of these!). If you find fewer than 50 such articles, expand your search to the preceding year.

3. Each member of your group should peruse the titles of the first 50 articles to get a sense of what they are about. For example, are they generally positive or negative? Are the themes of the stories similar? Do the articles concern the work of the profession with a specific population or problem? Next, read the text of 2 articles that interest you most, indicating on the Workspace worksheet the periodical in which each appeared, date of publication, title, and author. Print out one of them and staple it to your worksheet. [Note: often you will find that newspapers run the same stories, supplied to them by wire services. Make sure the articles you select differ from each other and are not the same story, run in two different papers.]

4. Answer the questions on the worksheets about both of the articles you have chosen.

5. This part of Workout 8 can be done on your own, for it requires doing something you probably already do: watch television! If you do not already do so, try to watch at least one television news program (CNN, Fox, ABC, CBS, NBC) per day for 10 days (to begin when instructed by your teacher). In addition, be on the lookout for any other news or "infotainment" program (e.g., *Dateline, 60 Minutes,* etc.) that previews a story likely to concern social work. Such a story may or may not air during the 10-day period specified by your instructor, but at least you will have seen it if it does. There may also be a storyline in a situation comedy or drama in which social work figures prominently. If so, try to watch that as well. Should any story, real or fictional, appear, address it in the Workspace.

WORKOUT 8 *Workspace*

Name _____

Date _____

1. The members of my group for this project were:

   _____

   _____

   _____

2. The news database used for this assignment was:

   _____

   _____

   _____

3. The number of articles printed this past year containing the words "social work" or "social worker" more than seven times was: _____

4. Of the 50 or so articles that you quickly perused, what were the most prevalent themes or ideas?

   _____

   _____

   _____

   _____

   _____

5. If you knew nothing about social work other than the ideas you picked up from your perusal of these articles, what would you think about this profession in terms of its purpose and mission?

   _____

   _____

_____

_____

_____

6. Consider more carefully the articles you have chosen.

   a. Name of periodical(s) in which   1. _____
      they appear:

                                      2. _____

   b. Dates of publication: 1. _____

                                        2. _____

   c. Titles of articles and authors: 1. _____

                                        2. _____

7. Briefly describe each article.

   Article 1:

_____

_____

_____

_____

_____

   Article 2:

_____

_____

_____

_____

_____

8. Select one of the two articles you discussed above for further analysis. Does this article provide a realistic, accurate image of the profession of social work? In what way? If not, how is it at odds with what you know about the social work profession?

_____

_____

_____

_____

9. Does the article make any assumptions about the profession that should be made explicit? For example, is it certain that the persons described as social workers in the article are, in fact, trained social workers? (One clue that they are not is if they are referred to by other titles, such as case manager or caseworker).

_____

_____

_____

_____

10. During the time period specified by your instructor, did you watch any television news or other programs that concerned social workers or the profession of social work? _____ Yes _____ No

11. If yes, what specific programs were they?

_____

_____

_____

_____

12. How did social work or social workers figure in the program?

_____

_____

_____

_____

13. Do you think the profession and its workers were fairly and accurately portrayed? If so, why? If not, why not?

_____

_____

_____

_____

14. If you saw a televised news story (either on an evening news program or on a newsmagazine show), what kinds of information were NOT given that would have made the story more complete and increased your understanding of what social workers do?

_____

_____

_____

_____

15. If the program you saw was a television drama, do you feel that the social worker as portrayed was a fair representation of professional social work behavior? If not, why not?

_____

_____

_____

_____

16. Finally, what did you learn from this assignment about the creation of an image through the media?

_____

_____

_____

_____

_____

WORKOUT 9   Clarifying Your Values

As both future social workers and moral human beings, we are driven to lead lives that express the values we hold closest to us. The values of the social work professional are explored in great detail in your text and need not be explicated here, except to say that respect for the dignity and inherent worth of the individual, self-determination, and a commitment to social justice are primary.

Rarely does one find any argument about values at this level. The problems arise over value conflicts/situations in which two value-based responses to the same problem are incompatible with each other. One of the roles our intellect plays is to help us determine which of the two responses is more justifiable, or preferable, in the face of this incompatibility.

A rapidly expanding field in which social workers may play a larger role in the future is that of biomedical ethics. Although only a relative few are trained in biomedical ethics specifically (it is apparently considered a branch of philosophy), ethics committees are forming in many places, particularly hospitals, as our expanding capacity to apply sophisticated medical technology to human problems runs up against our shrinking ability to pay for it for everyone who needs it. Ethics committees in these venues are given those terrible problems to resolve for which there are no good answers. Should a newborn with a very limited life expectancy be given expensive, painful treatments if they will prolong the baby's life a few more months? On what basis should a choice between two people on an organ transplant list be made when one organ becomes available? Must the social worker report the mother whose baby is born cocaine-addicted if the worker believes that the mother will then disappear and never ask for help again, further jeopardizing the baby's health?

It is these sorts of questions that we find most troubling and that our professional value base does not cover. It becomes important, then, to look at our personal values, for in the end it is those we rely on.

Location

In class

Purpose

1. To assist you in illuminating your own personal values.
2. To help you think about how and why one's values can be compromised.

Background

One of the things that I have found useful in crystallizing my own position on a given matter is having to defend it to someone else. If I find, in the course of my argument, that my position is not logically defensible, I either change my mind or come to recognize that I am wedded to my position, even though it may be logically weak, because it expresses a value that is of great importance to me.

In this workout, you may be asked to defend your position. Do your best, but listen to the competing ideas, too. What are the speakers really saying? Are they using logic or science to defend their position, or are they fighting values with values?

The relationship between science and values has always been a tenuous one and no more so than in social work. On the one hand, we are a normative profession that has been based in humanism; on the other, we are committed to finding, through scientific methods, ways to be better professionals. This workout should help you recognize how likely you are to use your values in your professional life.

Directions

1. The class divides into groups of about six persons each who are told that they have about 30 minutes to resolve the following situation.

   BEFORE BEGINNING THE DISCUSSION WITH GROUP MEMBERS, HOWEVER, TURN TO THE WORKSPACE AND ANSWER THE FIRST QUESTION INDEPENDENTLY. WHEN ALL MEMBERS OF YOUR GROUP HAVE DONE THAT, THE GROUP WORK MAY BEGIN.

2. You and the other members of your group serve on the Ethics Panel in a large hospital. The hospital was recently the recipient of a $1.5 million grant from a private foundation that stipulated that the money be used to obtain seven doses of a vaccine that reverses the course of AIDS and eventually rids the body entirely of the disease. The 14 people described briefly below all test positive for AIDS antibodies and wish to be vaccinated. You have been charged by the grant funders to decide which 7 of the 14 will be vaccinated. They also want to know that some systematic process has been implemented.

To come up with a group that is acceptable to as many group members as possible, you might wish to see if you can agree on some sort of hierarchy that may guide you in your decision making (i.e., should younger people be given preference over older? should past contributions to society be the most important, or potential contributions? should the number of dependents the candidates have be part of the equation? what about how they contracted the virus? etc.), or you may wish to decide on a case-by-case basis.

Candidates

1. A 15-year-old African American female was exposed to the virus through her 14-year-old boyfriend. She comes from a two-parent, middle-class family, attends junior high school, and is the fifth of nine children.

2. A 52-year-old White business executive and father of four, recently released from a federal penitentiary where he served two years for insider trading on the bond market, contracted the virus during a minor medical procedure in the prison hospital. Currently, he is doing 1,000 hours of community service teaching job skills and money management to inner-city youths.

3. A 35-year-old Hispanic mother of one child, 5 years of age, was exposed to the virus during an emergency blood transfusion. She has been happily married to her second husband for 3 years (her first husband, the girl's father, left the community and maintains no contact with either of them).

4. A 40-year-old single African United Nations refugee resettlement worker is responsible for placing thousands of refugee children from war-torn countries in permanent adoptive families. A member of an African tribe that practices polygamy, he was exposed to the virus through one of his mates. He has many children by a number of women.

5. A 23-year-old single White female is in training to become an Olympic athlete. Her family has made great sacrifices so that she might reach her full potential as an athlete. She is concerned that if she does not get the vaccine she will not be able to repay them for the sacrifices they have made.

6. A 38-year-old single Asian male is one of the few artists to have survived the persecution in his homeland and to perpetuate the artistic traditions of his people.

7. A 72-year-old mother, grandmother, and wife is the sole caretaker of her 76-year-old husband who has severe arthritis.

8. A 49-year-old White woman with four children (one of whom is developmentally disabled), is from an upper-middle-class background and was probably exposed to the virus during an extramarital affair.

9. A 56-year-old Hispanic male, with a wife and seven children, was also most likely exposed to the virus during an extramarital affair. He is a machinist and the sole support of his family.

10. A 20-year-old single college student majoring in education has no idea how she became exposed to the virus and has not told her family that she tests positive for HIV.
11. An 18-month-old baby was exposed to the virus through his mother, who has a full-blown case of AIDS. His father has already died of the disease.
12. A 49-year-old clergyman is the spiritual guide to the congregants of the largest church in the state. He has blessed thousands of babies, presided over hundreds of weddings and funerals, and provided solace and support to countless persons who needed it.
13. A 29-year-old househusband takes care of a house and three children while his wife attends medical school and works part-time as a lab technician.
14. A 56-year-old single White genetic researcher is close to completing work on finding a cure for diabetes, which has a good possibility of ultimately resulting in the perfection of a gene-altering procedure that would rid us of the scourge of diabetes.

[As you deliberate with your fellow group members, remember that there is no way around it: Seven of these folks are going to have to do without. This is not easy to contemplate, even hypothetically.]

3. Your teacher first asks a representative of each group to list the seven people chosen on the blackboard in columns across the board, so you can compare intragroup differences. Your instructor (or a class member) then leads the class as a whole in the discussion of the exercise, inviting groups to explain how they arrived at their decisions, dissenters within groups to articulate their opposing views, and spokespeople for each group to ask questions of members of other groups. [Note: No one individual or group should feel bad about the decisions they were forced to make. If you do not feel uncomfortable at some level about your decisions, something is wrong!] The values illuminated for each person as a result of this discussion should be contemplated.

WORKOUT 9 *Workspace*

1. Prior to deliberating as a group, list the seven people you would want to see receive this medicine (in as close to rank order as possible), using the number designations given the candidates.

_____   _____   _____   _____

_____   _____   _____

_____

2. In the space below, note any general principles your group will try to adhere to as it deliberates on the fate of these 14 people.

_____

_____

_____

_____

_____

_____

_____

_____

_____

3. Do you personally disagree with the group consensus? If so, how?

_____

_____

_____

_____

_____

_____

_____

_____

_____

4. Now, deliberating as a group, come to a consensus on the top seven and list them here:

_____   _____   _____

_____   _____   _____

_____

5. After the class discussion, examine your feelings. Even though you knew this workout had no basis in reality, what made you most uncomfortable about it? What, if anything, did you learn about yourself as a result?

WORKOUT 10 Examining the Impact of Religious Values on the Clients of Social Work

Old men without wives, old women without husbands, old people without children, young children without fathers—these four types of people are the most destitute and have no one to turn to for help. Whenever King Wen put benevolent measures into effect, he always gave them first consideration. The Book of Songs says:

> Happy are the rich;
> But have pity on the helpless.

Confucianism. Mencius. I.B.5

> Give the King thy justice, O God,
> And thy righteousness to the Royal Son!

> May he judge thy people with righteousness,
> And thy poor with justice!

> Let the mountains bear prosperity for the people,
> and the hills, in righteousness!

> May he defend the cause of the poor of the people,
> give deliverance to the needy,
> and crush the oppressor!

Judaism and Christianity. Psalm 72.1-4

The profession of social work is deeply rooted in religious traditions and ideals. From our earliest beginnings, with the development in 1882 of the Charity Organization Society, to the present time, we have looked to those often contradictory ideals (i.e., poverty as sin vs. nonjudgmentalism; stigmatizing the need for aid vs. upholding dignity and worth) not only to inform our responses to clients but also to guide us in who we choose to serve (the "worthy" poor, the oppressed). These contradictions (along with the emergence of other belief systems, such as Social Darwinism and capitalism) have mitigated a truly generous national response to the poor; yet we remain a society that recognizes its obligations to those without homes, food, jobs, love, and hope. Social work is one of the primary professions that takes as its central mission the fulfillment of this obligation.

Because of this, it is not surprising that one of the main reasons for choosing social work as a career has been religious belief (Popple & Leighninger, 1990), yet the relationship between the two can be difficult. This difficulty is illuminated most clearly in those instances where core religious beliefs and the core values of social work practice collide, as the following examples demonstrate:

- As a social worker of the Catholic faith in a local junior high school, you find yourself working with an eighth-grade girl, who, much to her consternation, is pregnant. After supporting her as she informed her parents of her plight, the family has decided that an abortion is the best alternative. They want your help in accessing those services. Given your faith, this is something you cannot do, and you refer the case to a co-worker. But you are deeply conflicted by the experience. Wasn't the referral to another worker, which you are obligated to do under the NASW Code of Ethics, abetting this family in its quest and therefore a sin in the eyes of God? Given that this is likely to happen again, can you even continue in this job?

- You are an evangelical Christian who has been taught that homosexuality is a sin against nature and God. Recently, you found work at an adoption agency that specializes in placing special-needs children in adoptive homes. Today, a homosexual couple came to the agency to initiate an adoption process. They have a stable relationship, financial security, and there is no state law or agency policy preventing placement. Nevertheless, you are extremely uncomfortable with the application.

- You are a social worker of the Jewish faith, working in a large hospital on the Cardiac Care Unit. Recently, a man was admitted with a severe myocardial infarction (heart attack). He required extensive services, which you provided and, in the course of his stay, you got to know him and his wife really well, although the fact of your Judaism never came up. Today, he invited you to take part in a prayer service in his room, to be attended by him, his wife, and his two children. Flattered to be asked to attend something so meaningful to the client and frankly not knowing exactly how to say no, you agreed. When you got to his room, you found that the expectation was that everyone would participate, reading something from the New Testament. You were asked to read a prayer that was, to say the least, inconsistent with your religious beliefs and then "to pray, in Jesus' name." You really do not want to do this but are concerned that to demur will seriously fray the relationship you have built with this client and which is so important to your work with him.

All of these situations have been reported either by students or by practicing social workers I have known. Taken together they point out the extent to which our professional lives may be fraught with these competing obligations to both our true selves and our clients.

This issue has less resonance for some people than for others. Nevertheless, it behooves all of us, at the beginning of our careers, to examine our religious or spiritual roots—the core of all of our assumptions—where they came from and how they informed our choice to look at social work as a professional option. In doing so, we allow ourselves to examine more clearly the question of how we are likely to resolve value conflicts involving religion or spirituality and practice like the ones noted above and whether or not there can be resolutions that satisfy both.

If you have not already done so, read the NASW Code of Ethics (available through the Internet at **http://www.naswdc.org/CODE.HTM**). Although the Code provides no answers to specific problems you might encounter, it is the general framework on which social workers rely as they attempt to find the answers to pressing dilemmas in practice. Any difficulties you may have with the requirements in the Code should be discussed with your instructor.

WORKOUT 10 *Instructions*

Location

In and outside class

Purpose

1. To enable the exploration of your own belief system or faith tradition and its prescriptions for helping those in need.
2. To assist in the illumination of the consonance (or dissonance) between the values of the profession and your own value system.

Background

The profession of social work possesses a unique set of core values. In varying degrees, these values differ from other helping professions (i.e., physicians, nurses, teachers, psychologists, and businesspersons), all of which possess, to some degree, different values than those of the general population (Abbott, 1988, cited in Morales & Sheafor, 1995; Horner & Whitbeck, 1991; Roberts, 1989). These are the core values delineated by the NASW in 1996:

Value: *Service*

Ethical Principle: *Social workers' primary goal is to help people in need and to address social problems.*

Social workers elevate service to others above self-interest. Social workers draw on their knowledge, values, and skills to help people in need and to address social problems. Social workers are encouraged to volunteer some portion of their professional skills with no expectation of significant financial return (pro bono service).

Value: *Social Justice*

Ethical Principle: *Social workers challenge social injustice.*

Social workers pursue social change, particularly with and on behalf of vulnerable and oppressed individuals and groups of people. Social workers' social change efforts are focused primarily on issues of poverty, unemployment, discrimination, and other forms of social injustice. These activities seek to promote sensitivity to and knowledge about oppression and cultural and ethnic diversity. Social workers strive to ensure access to needed information, services, and resources; equality of opportunity; and meaningful participation in decision making for all people.

Value: *Dignity and Worth of the Person*

Ethical Principle: *Social workers respect the inherent dignity and worth of the person.*

Social workers treat each person in a caring and respectful fashion, mindful of individual differences and cultural and ethnic diversity. Social workers promote clients' socially responsible self-determination. Social workers seek to enhance clients' capacity and opportunity to change and to address their own needs. Social workers are cognizant of their dual responsibility to clients and to the broader society. They seek to resolve conflicts between clients' interests and the broader society's interests in a socially responsible manner consistent with the values, ethical principles, and ethical standards of the profession.

Value: *Importance of Human Relationships*

Ethical Principle: *Social workers recognize the central importance of human relationships.*

Social workers understand that relationships between and among people are an important vehicle for change. Social workers engage people as partners in the helping process. Social workers seek to strengthen relationships among people in a purposeful effort to promote, restore, maintain, and enhance the well-being of individuals, families, social groups, organizations, and communities.

Value: *Integrity*

Ethical Principle: *Social workers behave in a trustworthy manner.*

Social workers are continually aware of the profession's mission, values, ethical principles, and ethical standards and practice in a manner consistent with them. Social workers act honestly and responsibly and promote ethical practices on the part of the organizations with which they are affiliated.

Value: *Competence*

Ethical Principle: *Social workers practice within their areas of competence and develop and enhance their professional expertise.*

Social workers continually strive to increase their professional knowledge and skills and apply them in practice. Social workers should aspire to contribute to the knowledge base in the profession.

Because everything that social workers do must be rooted in professional values, it is important for us to assess both our comfort level with those values and our ability to adhere to them. For example, one of the most basic values of the profession is the recognition of the dignity of the individual. This value requires us to serve the client with a maximum of skill and devotion, tailoring our service to that person's (or persons') specific needs. This value militates against stereotyping people, based on characteristics ascribed to a class of persons to which the client belongs. Yet, in our everyday life, we all do this. The question is, are we willing to work to suspend our belief in stereotypes so that we can convey respect to clients and serve them to the best our ability? And can we respect and appreciate their differences?

Another core value requires of us a willingness to keep personal feelings and needs separate from professional relationships. In his book on social work practice with involuntary clients, Ron Rooney (1992) discusses some of the consequences of failing to keep our personal feelings and professional objectivity separate. When we feel negatively toward clients, we are more likely to impose new mandates, or new contractual obligations, on clients before releasing them from their contract. As an example of this, he describes a situation in which a client whose child was in foster care purchased a pair of very expensive athletic shoes that she really could not afford as a gift for her son. The worker, who felt this action was emblematic of the client's extreme profligacy, wanted to impose additional parenting skill training on the client as a condition for getting her child back (it should also be noted that the mother was late in returning the child from weekend visits back to the foster home several times, which the worker and the foster mother thought very rude). This would have been an unfair imposition, as it was not in the original contract, a fact subsequently pointed out to the worker (R. Rooney, personal communication, 1996). This points to the need to continuously monitor our feelings about the client or client characteristics to ensure that we do not unfairly impede them in their goals.

That said, the converse is also true: Many of us are attracted to social work because we find that our personal values are syntonic with the profession. For example, those of us who have been victimized by stereotyping and other forms of oppression may subsequently commit ourselves to fighting that on behalf of others similarly victimized.

Although we are often too busy in our work lives to have the luxury of thinking about where our assumptions come from, and the ways in which they (consciously or unconsciously) pervade our thinking, as students you have the luxury of doing so and need to take advantage of this.

Directions

This workout is intended as a prelude for class discussion about values, both personal and practice. Examine the questions and write down some notes that will enable you to participate effectively in that discussion. Attach your notes to the literature to which you are responding to hand in to your instructor afterward.

WORKOUT 10 *Workspace*

Name _____

Date _____

1. Select a biblical passage, folk tale, fable, or parable that holds special meaning for you. This writing should be one that has informed your personal beliefs or values. Are the values inherent in this written piece consistent with the values of professional social work practice noted above? In what way?

_____

_____

_____

_____

_____

_____

_____

_____

_____

_____

_____

_____

_____

_____

_____

_____

_____

_____

_____

_____

_____

_____

_____

_____

_____

_____

_____

_____

2. Now, either select another passage from your own religious or cultural tradition or select a passage from another. Discuss this piece in terms of its view of how a community should care for its poor. Is it consistent with the values reflected in the way our welfare system currently operates? In what way?

_____

_____

_____

_____

_____

_____

_____

_____

_____

_____

_____

WORKOUT 11 Helping Clients Formulate Identity
Homosexuality

One of the strongest contributors to a sense of connectedness in the world is the knowledge that we are part of a family. The most fundamental institution in society is the family; its function is to support us, buffer us against outside stressors, and provide a base from which we move to integrate ourselves with the outside world. Our collective cultural belief in the importance of families is reflected in two commonly held notions: first, that when we behave in a laudatory way, we make our families proud. The word *mensch,* a Yiddish word that literally means "a credit to one's parents," is firmly entrenched in our lexicon. Becoming a mensch, and thus a positive reflection on our family, is very important to most of us. The second is the obverse: When we find ourselves in situations that would bring sadness or disappointment to our families, the pain that results from the realization that we have lost esteem in their eyes can be enormous.

If you are a gay or bisexual person who has "come out" to your family (or particularly if you have not come out) or have received such information from a family member or know someone who has gone through such an experience, you are probably well aware of the pain, guilt, sadness, or sense of loss that accompanies the "coming out" process. It can be extremely difficult to navigate and has resulted, for some, in permanent estrangement from their family.

Conversely, even though the "coming out" process can engender a crisis, it can also be a foundation for a deeper, better relationship with one's family, one that is based on honesty and authenticity (the sources listed at the end of this workout may be helpful in informing you of the dynamics of coming out).

Regardless of the field of service in social work that you choose to enter, you will inevitably work with a gay or bisexual client. Although the issues that bring you in contact with such clients often have nothing to do with their sexual orientation, it nevertheless behooves all of us to understand them both as unique individuals and as a class of persons experiencing a common struggle.

Thus, this exercise's purpose is to increase your understanding of what it means to be a gay man, lesbian woman, or bisexual by placing yourself within the context of an experience that is common to many and that may require the support of a good social worker.

Location

In class (preparation, if necessary, may be done outside class)

Purpose

1. To acquire a profound understanding of the impact of "coming out" in families.
2. To extend our appreciation and respect for human diversity, a primary requirement for social workers.

Background

For those of us who do not identify as gay, lesbian, or bisexual, it is difficult to understand the fear associated with this realization. This fear is grounded in some stark realities: Since sexual orientation is not specifically included in the Civil Rights Act as a characteristic that triggers specific protections to persons within that group, gay persons may be denied employment, housing, or public accommodations with impunity (unless they live in a locale that explicitly covers them in city or state nondiscrimination statutes). They may also be denied membership in, or ejected from, religious institutions that heretofore provided their spiritual underpinnings. Without the protection or support of the larger society, the importance of the family's response to the revelation that their loved one is gay is even more critical. P-FLAG (Parents, Family, and Friends of Lesbians and Gays) is a national organization consisting of friends and family who provide support to others with gay family members and to the gay community as well (for further information, contact them at [202] 638-4200, or write to P-FLAG, Ste. 1030, 1101 14th St. NW, Washington, DC 20005, or E-mail: info@pflag.org).

Social workers can help gay, lesbian, and bisexual people by supporting them and their families during the coming-out process. We can also help by working with society at large (an obligation reinforced in our Code of Ethics) to rid ourselves of the homophobia that serves to sustain discrimination and misunderstanding between gays and "straights" in our society.

Directions

1. In the Workout 11 Workspace, write a letter to your parent(s) (if you are a "traditional" student) or, if more appropriate, to your child, informing them that you are not straight. Those of you who are straight, however, may feel that you have an inadequate knowledge base on which to proceed. I would suggest doing one or both of the following to prepare for this assignment:

- Ask any openly gay friends that you may have if they would relate their coming out story to you. My experience is that most are quite willing to share their stories. Ask them what, if anything, was the scariest part. Were they worried about a particular parent? Grandparents? Siblings? Was the potential loss of financial support worrisome (from either an employer or a parent)? How did their family members react? Were they surprised by the reaction? And what is the status of their relationship today?

- Read about this process in advance. Listed below are some books that may be helpful. If you yourself are gay, lesbian, or bisexual, you may draw upon your own experience or the experiences of others you know. And you too may be interested in these readings (many of which can be ordered through Amazon.com at **http://wwwl.electriciti.com/unity/gaybooks/parenting.html**).

  Benkov, L. (1994). *Reinventing the family: The emerging story of lesbian and gay parents.* New York: Crown.

  Bernstein, R. (1995). *Straight parents, gay children: Keeping families together.* New York: Thunder's Mouth Press.

  Borhek, M. (1993). *Coming out to parents: A two-way survival guide for lesbians and gay men and their parents.* Cleveland, OH: Pilgrim Press.

  Cammermeyer, M. (with C. Fisher). (1994). *Serving in silence.* New York: Viking.

  Dew, R. F. (1994). *The family heart: A memoir of when our son came out.* Reading, MA: Addison-Wesley Longman.

  Jullion, J. (1985). *Long way home: The oddysey of a lesbian mother and her children.* San Francisco: Cleis Press.

  Louganis, G. (with Eric Marcus). (1995). *Breaking the surface.* New York: Random House.

  Monette, P. (1992). *Becoming a man: Half a life story.* New York: Harcourt Brace Jovanovich.

  Wirth, M., Wirth, A., & Griffin, C. (1996). *Beyond acceptance: Parents of lesbians and gays talk about their experiences.* New York: St. Martin's.

2. You have 30 to 40 minutes to complete your letter. Then, **EXCHANGE** letters with another class member. Read that person's letter and respond, in writing, as if you were the recipient of the letter. State your own feelings and opinions. You have approximately 20 to 30 minutes to complete this task. (Note: You need not give your response to the person who wrote you the original letter.)

3. Your instructor now facilitates a discussion about this process: what you learned, what it felt like to "reveal" yourself, and what you hope has been the response to the letter. Willing persons should share their responses with the person with whom they exchanged letters. Reactions to those letters should be shared in the class as well.

WORKOUT 11 *Workspace*

Name _____

Date _____

Dear _____ :

_____

_____

_____

_____

_____

_____

_____

_____

_____

_____

_____

_____

_____

_____

_____

_____

_____

_____

_____

_____

_____

_____

_____

_____

_____

_____

_____

_____

_____

_____

_____

_____

_____

_____

_____

_____

_____

_____

_____

_____

_____

Love,

Your _____ (son, daughter, mother, father)

WORKOUT 12 Leading Clients From Oppression to Empowerment

It is fortunate for those of us engaged in social work practice that we need not have actually experienced every problem that our clients have experienced in order to be effective practitioners. Empathy, or the skill of identifying at a feeling level with the experiences or character of another person, spares us this impossible task. For example, you may have grown up in a loving, stable home. However, even in the best families, members may experience at some point pain, chaos, and instability. Those experiences allow you to identify with others who are also feeling these things, even though the experience producing the feelings is entirely different. Knowing how others feel has a profound impact on how you are likely to respond to them.

The experience of oppression is a common one in our culture, and it is particularly important for social workers to understand this experience because so many of our clients have been victimized by oppression. Persons of color, persons from minority cultures or religions, and gay men and lesbian women often have, as an integral part of their life history, stories of undue hardship, cruelty from the dominant culture, and injustice, which occurred because of their minority status.

There is an extensive body of literature that explores the psychology of oppression, too detailed to articulate fully here, but which has been neatly summarized by Shulman (1992). Drawing on the work of Fanon (1968), Bulhan (1985), and Hegel (1807/1966), Shulman shows how prolonged exposure to oppression may lead clients to internalize the "oppressor without," adopting the oppressor's negative stereotypes and images of them. Such clients become "autoppressors" by participating in their own oppression and self-hate. Malcolm X, in his autobiography, gives us a striking example of this in his account of how he, as a young man, "conked" his hair, replacing his own dark, "kinky" color and texture with straight, reddish hair, in a futile attempt to look more like the White man (his oppressor). The fact that the process involved the direct application of lye to the head, which produces a very painful, burning sensation, simply provides more evidence of the power of autoppression. Similarly, observations of women's very low self-esteem when they first come to a shelter for battered women exemplifies how women may come to adopt as their own the negative messages they receive about themselves from the batterer.

Bulhan (1985) writes that oppressed persons employ different ego defenses in their struggle (*compromise, flight,* and *fight*) and that these struggles are implemented in stages: capitulation (or autoppression), revitalization (or the embrace of the indigenous culture), and radicalization (the individual commits to the struggle for radical change). Although this model most directly applies to racial and cultural oppression, it can have application to other instances of defensive reactions to oppression.

Most social workers find these concepts useful for understanding clients who have lived under conditions of prolonged oppression. Clearly, they normalize clients' lives and responses to their situations.

However, what should not be overlooked is the resilience of many people who exist under extremely oppressive conditions yet find ways to rise above these conditions and even prosper, as the following examples illustrate. Read what they have to say and see if you agree.

WORKOUT 12 *Instructions*

Location

In class, with outside preparation time

Purpose

1. To learn how to critically analyze reactions to oppression by members of oppressed groups, and to apply this knowledge to the principles of social work practice.
2. To illuminate the concept of resiliency among members of oppressed groups.

Background

The pieces to be read for this exercise illuminate the experiences of people who have overcome considerable odds and write movingly about the process. The first, Gertrude Simmons Bonnin (1876-1938), was also known as Zitkala-Sa. As she recounts in her autobiographical work, excerpted here, she was raised as a Yankton Sioux until she was sent to a Quaker missionary school for Indians in Indiana. This experience was likely the crucible of her life and provided the force behind her prodigious efforts to improve the lives of other Native peoples through legislative reform. She was involved with the Society of American Indians (established in 1911) and was elected its secretary in 1916. She founded the Indian Welfare Committee of the General Federation of Women's Clubs in 1921. In cooperation with the Indian Rights Association, the federation was successful in improving the treatment of Native peoples and preserving their culture. Bonnin's social reform work left her little time for writing—only two books. But the quality of the work is undeniable.

Kay Redfield Jamison was born into a military family; her father was a colonel in the Air Force and a meteorologist with the Air Weather Service. When she was 15, her father retired and moved the family from a military environment in Washington, D.C., to southern California. Deeply unhappy, she watched her father sink deeper and deeper into serious depressions. By the time she was 16 or 17, she too had begun to experience the swings of Manic-Depressive Disorder that would escalate into flights of suicidal thoughts and behavior counterbalanced by manic episodes that found her spending large sums of money and exhausting everyone around her. Ultimately, her illness would be controlled by lithium, but it is instructive to note that, while she is currently Professor of Psychiatry at Johns Hopkins School of Medicine and one of the foremost authorities on manic-depressive illness, even she had difficulty accepting the realization that she would require medication for the rest of her life.

Tobias Wolff is considered one of our finest contemporary memoirists. Raised around the Northwest by a mother who had extreme difficulty making ends meet (and without the child support owed by his father), Wolff was forced to spend significant amounts of time with Roy, his mother's boyfriend, and then Dwight, his rather sadistic and unstable stepfather. Wolff is masterful at evoking the skills of survival in an environment that robs so many children of their sense of worth and agency.

Nancy Mairs calls herself a "Catholic feminist" writer, and many of her essays focus on how she makes sense of (by her definition) these two seemingly incompatible worldviews. Stricken with multiple sclerosis as a young adult and now very restricted in her mobility, Mairs beautifully and intelligently evokes for us what it is like to be "waist-high in the world" and how the support of her family has been so indispensable to her productivity and quality of life.

Mary Crow Dog is a Sioux Indian from the Rosebud Reservation in South Dakota, one of the poorest communities in the country. Sent to Indian boarding school as a young girl, Mary Crow Dog drank heavily from the time she was 10 until she became a mother, apparently in her teens. Married to Leonard Crow Dog, Mary was able to survive the Battle of Wounded Knee and gives one of the most harrowing accounts of that battle ever written. Her point of view as a woman, and particularly as a woman giving birth while the battle was raging around her, is extremely vivid and detailed. Her book, *Lakota Woman,* from which this excerpt is taken, not only relates how she was able to transform herself into a fighter and a survivor but provides a pathway to understanding the vast chasm between Native Americans and Caucasians and offers some clues for how to bridge that gap.

How is it that each of these people was able to find his or her way in environments that were oppressive, inhospitable, or (in the case of Jamison) simply overwhelming? Perhaps these pieces can give us clues as to the special qualities we may need to help clients develop so that they too can make their way in the world.

Directions

1. Read the literary selections by Bonnin, Jamison, Wolff, Mairs, and/or (depending on the instructions of your teacher) Crow Dog reprinted below. Your instructor may wish to have you read only one or all of them. The work can be modified to fit the needs of the class.

2. Answer the questions in the Workspace.

3. Your instructor will discuss the readings and the questions with the class as a whole prior to your turning in your assignment.

Impressions of an Indian Girlhood

by Zitkala-Sa

VII.   The Big Red Apples

The first turning away from the easy, natural flow of my life occurred in an early spring. It was in my eighth year; in the month of March, I afterward learned. At this age I knew but one language, and that was my mother's native tongue.

From some of my playmates I heard that two paleface missionaries were in our village. They were from that class of white men who wore big hats and carried large hearts, they said. Running direct to my mother, I began to question her why these two strangers were among us. She told me, after I had teased much, that they had come to take away Indian boys and girls to the East. My mother did not seem to want me to talk about them. But in a day or two, I gleaned many wonderful stories from my playfellows concerning the strangers.

"Mother, my friend Judewin is going home with the missionaries. She is going to a more beautiful country than ours; the palefaces told her so!" I said wistfully, wishing in my heart that I too might go.

Mother sat in a chair, and I was hanging on her knee. Within the last two seasons my big brother Dawee had returned from a three years' education in the East, and his coming back influenced my mother to take a farther step from her native way of living. First it was a change from the buffalo skin to the white man's canvas that covered our wigwam. Now she had given up her wigwam of slender poles, to live, a foreigner, in a home of clumsy logs.

"Yes, my child, several others besides Judewin are going away with the palefaces. Your brother said the missionaries had inquired about his little sister," she said, watching my face very closely.

My heart thumped so hard against my breast, I wondered if she could hear it.

"Did he tell them to take me, mother?" I asked, fearing lest Dawee had forbidden the palefaces to see me, and that my hope of going to the Wonderland would be entirely blighted.

With a sad, slow smile, she answered: "There! I knew you were wishing to go, because Judewin has filled your ears with the white men's lies. Don't believe a word they say! Their words are sweet, but, my child, their deeds are bitter. You will cry for me, but they will not even soothe you. Stay with me, my little one! Your brother Dawee says that going East, away from your mother, is too hard an experience for his baby sister."

Thus my mother discouraged my curiosity about the lands beyond our eastern horizon; for it was not yet an ambition for Letters that was stirring me. But on the following day the missionaries did come to our very house. I spied them coming up the footpath leading to our cottage. A third man was with them, but he was not my brother Dawee. It was another, a young interpreter, a paleface who had a smattering of the Indian language. I was ready to run out to meet them, but I did not dare to displease my mother. With great glee, I jumped up and down on our ground floor. I begged my mother to open the door, that they would be sure to come to us. Alas! They came, they saw, and they conquered!

Judewin had told me of the great tree where grew red, red apples; and how we could reach out our hands and pick all the red apples we could eat. I had never seen apple trees. I had never tasted more than a dozen red apples in my life, and when I heard of the orchards of the East, I was eager to roam among them. The missionaries smiled into my eyes, and patted my head. I wondered how mother could say such hard words against them.

"Mother, ask them if little girls may have all the red apples they want, when they go East," I whispered aloud, in my excitement.

The interpreter heard me, and answered: "Yes, little girl, the nice red apples are for those who pick them; and you will have a ride on the iron horse if you go with these good people."

I had never seen a train, and he knew it.

"Mother, I'm going East! I like big red apples, and I want to ride on the iron horse! Mother, say yes!" I pleaded.

My mother said nothing. The missionaries waited in silence; and my eyes began to blur with tears, though I struggled to choke them back. The corners of my mouth twitched, and my mother saw me.

"I am not ready to give you any word," she said to them. "To-morrow I shall send you my answer by my son."

With this they left us. Alone with my mother, I yielded to my tears, and cried aloud, shaking my head so as not to hear what she was saying to me. This was the first time I had ever been so unwilling to give up my own desire that I refused to hearken to my mother's voice.

There was a solemn silence in our home that night. Before I went to bed I begged the Great Spirit to make my mother willing I should go with the missionaries.

The next morning came, and my mother called me to her side. "My daughter, do you still persist in wishing to leave your mother?" she asked.

"Oh, mother, it is not that I wish to leave you, but I want to see the wonderful Eastern land," I answered.

My dear old aunt came to our house that morning, and I heard her say, "Let her try it."

I hoped that, as usual, my aunt was pleading on my side. My brother Dawee came for mother's decision. I dropped my play and crept close to my aunt.

"Yes, Dawee, my daughter, though she does not understand what it all means, is anxious to go. She will need an education when she is grown, for then there will be fewer real Dakotas, and many more palefaces. This tearing her away, so young, from her mother is necessary, if I would have her an educated woman. The palefaces, who owe us a large debt for stolen lands, have begun to pay a tardy justice in offering some education to our children. But I know my daughter must suffer keenly in this experiment. For her sake, I dread to tell you my reply to the missionaries. Go, tell them that they may take my little daughter, and that the Great Spirit shall not fail to reward them according to their hearts."

Wrapped in my heavy blanket, I walked with my mother to the carriage that was soon to take us to the iron horse. I was happy. I met my playmates, who were also wearing their best thick blankets. We showed one another our new beaded moccasins and the width of the belts that girdled our new dresses. Soon we were being drawn rapidly away by the white man's horses. When I saw the lonely figure of my mother vanish in the distance, a sense of regret settled heavily upon me. I felt suddenly weak, as if I might fall limp to the ground. I was in the hands of strangers whom my mother did not fully trust. I no longer felt free to be myself or to voice my own feelings. The tears trickled down my cheeks, and I buried my face in the folds of my blanket. Now the first step, parting me from my mother, was taken, and all my belated tears availed nothing.

Having driven thirty miles to the ferryboat, we crossed the Missouri in the evening. Then riding again a few miles eastward, we stopped before a massive brick building. I looked at it in amazement, and with a vague misgiving, for in our village I had never seen so large a house. Trembling with fear and distrust of the palefaces, my teeth chattering from the chilly ride, I crept noiselessly in my soft moccasins along the narrow hall, keeping very close to the bare wall. I was as frightened and bewildered as the captured young of a wild creature.

The School Days of an Indian Girl

by Zitkala-Sa

I.   The Land of Red Apples

There were eight in our party of bronzed children who were going East with the missionaries. Among us were three young braves, two tall girls, and we three little ones, Judewin, Thowin, and I.

We had been very impatient to start on our journey to the Red Apple Country, which, we were told, lay a little beyond the great circular horizon of the Western prairie. Under a sky of rosy apples we dreamt of roaming as freely and happily as we had chased the cloud shadows on the Dakota plains. We had anticipated much pleasure from a ride on the iron horse, but the throngs of staring palefaces disturbed and troubled us.

On the train, fair women, with tottering babies on each arm, stopped their haste and scrutinized the children of absent mothers. Large men, with heavy bundles in their hands, halted near by, and riveted their glassy blue eyes upon us.

I sank deep into the corner of my seat, for I resented being watched. Directly in front of me, children who were no larger than I hung themselves upon the backs of their seats, with their bold white faces toward me. Sometimes they took their forefingers out of their mouths and pointed at my moccasined feet. Their mothers, instead of reproving such rude curiosity, looked closely at me and attracted their children's further notice to my blanket. This embarrassed me and kept me constantly on the verge of tears.

I sat perfectly still, with my eyes downcast, daring only now and then to shoot long glances around me. Chancing to turn to the window at my side, I was quite breathless upon seeing one familiar object. It was the telegraph pole which strode by at short paces. Very near my mother's dwelling, along the edge of a road thickly bordered with wild sunflowers, some poles like these had been planted by white men. Often I had stopped, on my way down the road to hold my ear against the pole, and, hearing its low moaning, I used to wonder what the paleface had done to hurt it. Now I sat watching for each pole that glided by to be the last one.

In this way I had forgotten my uncomfortable surroundings, when I heard one of my comrades call out my name. I saw the missionary standing very near, tossing candies and gum into our midst. This amused us all, and we tried to see who could catch the most of the sweetmeats. The missionary's generous distribution of candies was impressed upon my memory by a disastrous result which followed. I had caught more than my share of candies and gum, and soon after our arrival at the school I had a chance to disgrace myself, which, I am ashamed to say, I did.

Though we rode several days inside of the iron horse, I do not recall a single thing about our luncheons.

It was night when we reached the school grounds. The lights from the windows of the large buildings fell upon some of the icicled trees that stood beneath them. We were led toward an open door, where the brightness of the lights within flooded out over the heads of the excited palefaces who blocked the way. My body trembled more from fear than from the snow I trod upon.

Entering the house, I stood close against the wall. The strong glaring light in the large whitewashed room dazzled my eyes. The noisy hurrying of hard shoes upon a bare wooden floor increased the whirring in my ears. My only safety seemed to be in keeping next to the wall. As I was wondering in which direction to escape from all this confusion, two warm hands grasped me firmly, and in the same moment I was tossed high in midair. A rosy-checked paleface woman caught me in her arms. I was both frightened and insulted by such trifling. I stared into her eyes, wishing her to let me stand on my own feet, but she jumped me up and down with increasing enthusiasm. My mother had never made a plaything of her wee daughter. Remembering this I began to cry aloud.

They misunderstood the cause of my tears and placed me at a white table loaded with food. There our party were united again. As I did not hush my crying, one of the older ones whispered to me, "Wait until you are alone in the night."

It was very little I could swallow besides my sobs that evening

"Oh, I want my mother and my brother Dawee. I want to go to my aunt!" I pleaded; but the ears of the palefaces could not hear me.

From the table we were taken along an upward incline of wooden boxes, which I learned afterward to call a stairway. At the top was a quiet hall, dimly lighted. Many narrow beds were in one straight line down the entire length of the wall. In them lay sleeping brown faces, which peeped just out of the coverings. I was tucked into bed with one of the tall girls, because she talked to me in my mother tongue and seemed to soothe me.

I had arrived in the wonderful land of rosy skies, but I was not happy, as I had thought I should be. My long travel and the bewildering sights had exhausted me. I fell asleep, heaving deep, tired sobs. My tears were left to dry themselves in streaks, because neither my aunt nor my mother was near to wipe them away.

II. The Cutting of My Long Hair

The first day in the land of apples was a bitter-cold one, for the snow still covered the ground, and the trees were bare. A large bell rang for breakfast, its loud metallic voice crashing through the belfry overhead and into our sensitive ears. The annoying clatter of shoes on bare floors gave us no peace. The constant clash of harsh noises, with an undercurrent of many voices murmuring an unknown tongue, made a bedlam within which I was securely tied. And though my spirit tore itself in struggling for its lost freedom, all was useless.

A paleface woman, with white hair, came up after us. We were placed in a line of girls who were marching into the dining room. These were Indian girls, in stiff shoes and closely clinging dresses. The small girls wore sleeved aprons and shingled hair. As I walked noiselessly in my soft moccasins, I felt like sinking to the floor, for my blanket had been stripped from my shoulders. I looked hard at the Indian girls, who seemed not to care that they were even more immodestly dressed than I, in their tightly fitting clothes. While we marched in, the boys entered at an opposite door. I watched for the three young braves who came in our party. I spied them in the rear ranks, looking as uncomfortable as I felt.

A small bell was tapped, and each of the pupils drew a chair from under the table. Supposing this act meant they were to be seated, I pulled out mine and at once slipped into it from one side. But when I turned my head, I saw that I was the only one seated, and all the rest at our table remained standing. Just as I began to rise, looking shyly around to see how chairs were to be used, a second bell was sounded. All were seated at last, and I had to crawl back into my chair again. I heard a man's voice at one end of the hall, and I looked around to see him. But all the others hung their heads over their plates. As I glanced at the long chain of tables, I caught the eyes of a paleface woman upon me. Immediately I dropped my eyes, wondering why I was so keenly watched by the strange woman. The man ceased his mutterings, and then a third bell was tapped. Every one picked up his knife and fork and began eating. I began crying instead, for by this time I was afraid to venture anything more.

But this eating by formula was not the hardest trial in that first day. Late in the morning, my friend Judewin gave me a terrible warning. Judewin knew a few words of English; and she had overheard the paleface woman talk about cutting our long, heavy hair. Our mothers had taught us that only unskilled warriors who were captured had their hair shingled by the enemy. Among our people, short hair was worn by mourners and shingled hair by cowards!

We discussed our fate some moments, and when Judewin said, "We have to submit because they are strong," I rebelled.

"No, I will not submit! I will struggle first!" I answered.

I watched my chance, and when no one noticed I disappeared. I crept up the stairs as quietly as I could in my squeaking shoes—my moccasins had been exchanged for shoes. Along the hall I passed, without knowing whither I was going. Turning aside to an open door, I found a large room with three white beds in it. The windows were covered with dark green curtains, which made the room very dim. Thankful that no one was there, I directed my steps toward the corner farthest from the door. On my hands and knees I crawled under the bed and cuddled myself in the dark corner.

From my hiding place I peered out, shuddering with fear whenever I heard footsteps nearby. Though in the hall loud voices were calling my name, and I knew that even Judewin was searching for me, I did not open my mouth to answer. Then the steps were quickened and the voices became excited. The sounds came nearer and nearer. Women and girls entered the room. I held my breath, and watched them open closet doors and peep behind large trunks. Someone threw up the curtains, and the room was filled with sudden light. What caused them to stoop and look under the bed I do not know. I remember being dragged out, though I resisted by kicking and scratching wildly. In spite of myself, I was carried downstairs and tied fast in a chair.

I cried aloud, shaking my head all the while until I felt the cold blades of the scissors against my neck, and heard them gnaw off one of my thick braids. Then I lost my spirit. Since the day I was taken from my mother I had suffered extreme indignities. People had stared at me. I had been tossed about in the air like a wooden puppet. And now my long hair was shingled like a coward's! In my anguish I moaned for my mother, but no one came to comfort me. Not a soul reasoned quietly with me, as my own mother used to do; for now I was only one of many little animals driven by a herder.

III. The Snow Episode

A short time after our arrival we three Dakotas were playing in the snowdrifts. We were all still deaf to the English language, excepting Judewin, who always heard such puzzling things. One morning we learned through her ears that we were forbidden to fall lengthwise in the snow, as we had been doing, to see our own impressions. However, before many hours we had forgotten the order, and were having great sport in the snow, when a shrill voice called us.

Looking up, we saw an imperative hand beckoning us into the house. We shook the snow off ourselves and started toward the woman as slowly as we dared.

Judewin said, "Now the paleface is angry with us. She is going to punish us for falling into the snow. If she looks straight into your eyes and talks loudly, you must wait until she stops. Then, after a tiny pause, say, 'No.' " The rest of the way we practiced upon the little word "no."

As it happened, Thowin was summoned to judgment first. The door shut behind her with a click.

Judewin and I stood silently listening at the keyhole. The paleface woman talked in very severe tones. Her words fell from her lips like crackling embers, and her inflection ran up like the small end of a switch. I understood her voice better than the things she was saying. I was certain we had made her very impatient with us. Judewin heard enough of the words to realize all too late that she had taught us the wrong reply.

"Oh, poor Thowin!" she gasped, as she put both hands over her ears.

Just then I heard Thowin's tremulous answer, "No."

With an angry exclamation, the woman gave her a hard spanking. Then she stopped to say something. Judewin said it was this: "Are you going to obey my word the next time?"

Thowin answered again with the only word at her command, "No."

This time the woman meant her blows to smart, for the poor frightened girl shrieked at the top of her voice. In the midst of the whipping the blows ceased abruptly, and the woman asked another question: "Are you going to fall in the snow again?"

Thowin gave her bad password another trial. We heard her say feebly, "No."

With this the woman hid away her half-worn slipper, and led the child out stroking her black shorn head. Perhaps it occurred to her that brute force is not the solution for such a problem. She did nothing to Judewin nor to me. She only returned to us our unhappy comrade and left us alone in the room.

During the first two or three seasons misunderstandings as ridiculous as this one of the snow episode frequently took place, bringing unjustifiable frights and punishments into our little lives.

Within a year I was able to express myself somewhat in broken English. As soon as I comprehended a part of what was said and done, a mischievous spirit of revenge possessed me. One day I was called in from my play for some misconduct. I had disregarded a rule which seemed to me very needlessly binding. I was sent into the kitchen to mash the turnips for dinner. It was noon, and steaming dishes were hastily carried into the dining room. I hated turnips, and their odor which came from the brown jar was offensive to me. With fire in my heart, I took the wooden tool that the paleface woman held out to me. I stood upon a step, and, grasping the handle with both hands, I bent in hot rage over the turnips. I worked my vengeance upon them. All were so busily occupied that no one noticed me. I saw that the turnips were in a pulp, and that further beating could not improve them; but the order was "Mash these turnips," and mash them I would! I renewed my energy, and as I sent the masher into the bottom of the jar, I felt a satisfying sensation that the weight of my body had gone into it.

Just then a paleface woman came up to my table. As she looked into the jar, she shoved my hands roughly aside. I stood fearless and angry. She placed her red hands upon the rim of the jar. Then she gave one lift and a stride away from the table. But lo! the pulpy contents fell through the crumbled bottom to the floor! She spared me no scolding phrases that I had earned. I did not heed them. I felt triumphant in my revenge, though deep within me I was a wee bit sorry to have broken the jar.

As I sat eating my dinner and saw that no turnips were served, I whooped in my heart for having once asserted the rebellion within me.

IV. The Devil

Among the legends the old warriors used to tell me were many stories of evil spirits. But I was taught to fear them no more than those who stalked about in maternal guise. I never knew there was an insolent chieftain among the bad spirits, who dared to array his forces against the Great Spirit, until I heard this white man's legend from a paleface woman.

Out of a large book she showed me a picture of the white man's devil. I looked in horror upon the strong claws that grew out of his fur-covered fingers. His feet were like his hands. Trailing at his heels was a scaly tail tipped with a serpent's open jaws. His face was a patchwork: he had bearded cheeks, like some I had seen palefaces wear, his nose was an eagle's bill, and his sharp-pointed ears were pricked up like those of a sly fox. Above them a pair of cow's horns curved upward. I trembled with awe, and my heart throbbed in my throat as I looked at the king of evil spirits. Then I heard the paleface woman say that this terrible creature roamed loose in the world, and that little girls who disobeyed school regulations were to be tortured by him.

That night I dreamt about this evil divinity. Once again I seemed to be in my mother's cottage. An Indian woman had come to visit my mother. On opposite sides of the kitchen stove, which stood in the center of the small house, my mother and her guest were seated in straight-backed chairs. I played with a train of empty spools hitched together on a string. It was night, and the wick burned feebly. Suddenly I heard someone turn our doorknob from without.

My mother and the woman hushed their talk, and both looked toward the door. It opened gradually. I waited behind the stove. The hinges squeaked as the door was slowly, very slowly pushed inward.

Then in rushed the devil! He was tall! He looked exactly like the picture I had seen of him in the white man's papers. He did not speak to my mother because he did not know the Indian language, but his glittering yellow eyes were fastened upon me. He took long strides around the stove, passing behind the woman's chair. I threw down my spools and ran to my mother. He did not fear her but followed closely after me. Then I ran round and round the stove, crying aloud for help. But my mother and the woman seemed not to know my danger. They sat still, looking quietly upon the devil's chase after me. At last I grew dizzy. My head revolved as on a hidden pivot. My knees became numb and doubled under my weight like a pair of knife blades without a spring. Beside my mother's chair I fell in a heap. Just as the devil stooped over me with outstretched claws my mother awoke from her quiet indifference and lifted me on her lap, whereupon the devil vanished and I was awake.

On the following morning I took my revenge upon the devil. Stealing into the room where a wall of shelves was filled with books, I drew forth *The Stories of the Bible*. With a broken slate pencil I carried in my apron pocket, I began by scratching out his wicked eyes. A few moments later, when I was ready to leave the room, there was a ragged hole in the page where the picture of the devil had once been.

V. Iron Routine

A loud-clamoring bell awakened us at half past six in the cold winter mornings. From happy dreams of Western rolling lands and unlassoed freedom we tumbled out upon chilly bare floors back again into a paleface day. We had a short time to jump into our shoes and clothes and wet our eyes with icy water before a small hand bell was vigorously rung for roll call.

There were too many drowsy children and too numerous orders for the day to waste a moment in any apology to nature for giving her children such a shock in the early morning. We rushed downstairs, bounding over two high steps at a time, to land in the assembly room.

A paleface woman, with a yellow-covered roll book open on her arm and a gnawed pencil in her hand, appeared at the door. Her small, tired face was coldly lighted with a pair of large gray eyes.

She stood still in a halo of authority, while over the rim of her spectacles her eyes pried nervously about the room. Having glanced at her long list of names and called out the first one, she tossed up her chin and peered through the crystals of her spectacles to make sure of the answer "Here."

Relentlessly her pencil black-marked our daily records if we were not present to respond to our names, and no chum of ours had done it successfully for us. No matter if a dull headache or the painful cough of slow consumption had delayed the absentee, there was only time enough to mark the tardiness. It was next to impossible to leave the iron routine after the civilizing machine had once begun its day's buzzing; and as it was inbred in me to suffer in silence rather than to appeal to the ears of one whose open eyes could not see my pain, I have many times trudged in the day's harness heavy-footed, like a dumb sick brute.

Once I lost a dear classmate. I remember well how she used to mope along at my side, until one morning she could not raise her head from her pillow. At her deathbed I stood weeping, as the paleface woman sat near her moistening the dry lips. Among the folds of the bedclothes I saw the open pages of the white man's Bible. The dying Indian girl talked disconnectedly of Jesus the Christ and the paleface who was cooling her swollen hands and feet.

I grew bitter and censured the woman for cruel neglect of our physical ills. I despised the pencils that moved automatically, and the one teaspoon which dealt out, from a large bottle, healing to a row of variously ailing Indian children. I blamed the hard-working, well-meaning, ignorant woman who was inculcating in our hearts her superstitious ideas. Though I was sullen in all my little troubles, as soon as I felt better I was ready again to smile upon the cruel woman. Within a week I was again actively testing the chains which tightly bound my individuality like a mummy for burial.

The melancholy of those black days has left so long a shadow that it darkens the path of years that have since gone by. These sad memories rise above those of smoothly grinding school days. Perhaps my Indian nature is the moaning wind which stirs them now for their present record. But, however tempestuous this is within me, it comes out as the low voice of a curiously colored seashell, which is only for those ears that are bent with compassion to hear it.

VI. Four Strange Summers

After my first three years of school, I roamed again in the Western country through four strange summers.

During this time I seemed to hang in the heart of chaos, beyond the touch or voice of human aid. My brother, being almost ten years my senior, did not understand my feelings. My mother had never gone inside of a schoolhouse, and so she was not capable of comforting her daughter who could read and write. Even nature seemed to have no place for me. I was neither a wee girl nor a tall one, neither a wild Indian nor a tame one. This deplorable situation was the effect of my brief course in the East, and the unsatisfactory "teens" in a girl's years.

It was under these trying conditions that, one bright afternoon, as I sat restless and unhappy in my mother's cabin, I caught the sound of the spirited step of my brother's pony on the road which passed by our dwelling. Soon I heard the wheels of a light buckboard, and Dawee's familiar "Ho!" to his pony. He alighted upon the bare ground in front of our house. Tying his pony to one of the projecting corner logs of the low-roofed cottage, he stepped up on the wooden doorstep.

I met him there with a hurried greeting, and, as I passed by, he looked a quiet "What?" into my eyes.

When he began talking with my mother, I slipped the rope from the pony's bridle. Seizing the reins and bracing my feet against the dashboard, I wheeled around in an instant. The pony was ever ready to try his speed. Looking backward, I saw Dawee waving his hand to me. I turned with the curve in the road and disappeared. I followed the winding road which crawled upward between the bases of little hillocks. Deep water-worn ditches ran parallel on either side A strong wind blew against my cheeks and fluttered my sleeves. The pony reached the top of the highest hill and began an even race on the level lands.

There was nothing moving within that great circular horizon of the Dakota prairies save the tall grasses, over which the wind blew and rolled off in long shadowy waves.

Within this vast wigwam of blue and green I rode reckless and insignificant. It satisfied my small consciousness to see the white foam fly from the pony's mouth.

Suddenly, out of the earth a coyote came forth at a swinging trot that was taking the cunning thief toward the hills and the village beyond. Upon the moment's impulse, I gave him a long chase and a wholesome fright. As I turned away to go back to the village, the wolf sank down upon his haunches for rest, for it was a hot summer day, and as I drove slowly homeward I saw his sharp nose pointed at me, until I vanished below the margin of the hilltops. In a little while I came in sight of my mother's house. Dawee stood in the yard, laughing at an old warrior who was pointing his forefinger, and again waving his whole hand, toward the hills. With his blanket drawn over one shoulder, he talked and motioned excitedly. Dawee turned the old man by the shoulder and pointed me out to him.

"Oh hen!" (Oh yes) the warrior muttered, and went his way. He had climbed to the top of his favorite barren hill to survey the surrounding prairies, when he spied my chase after the coyote. His keen eyes recognized the pony and driver At once uneasy for my safety, he had come running to my mother's cabin to give her warning. I did not appreciate his kindly interest, for there was an unrest gnawing at my heart.

As soon as he went away, I asked Dawee about something else.

"No, my baby sister, I cannot take you with me to the party tonight," he replied. Though I was not far from fifteen and I felt that before long I should enjoy all the privileges of my tall cousin, Dawee persisted in calling me his baby sister.

That moonlight night, I cried in my mother's presence when I heard the jolly young people pass by our cottage. They were no more young braves in blankets and eagle plumes, nor Indian maids with prettily painted cheeks. They had gone three years to school in the East and had become civilized. The young men wore the white man's coat and trousers, with bright neckties. The girls wore tight muslin dresses, with ribbons at neck and waist. At these gatherings they talked English. I could speak English almost as well as my brother, but I was not properly dressed to be taken along. I had no hat, no ribbons, and no close-fitting gown. Since my return from school I had thrown away my shoes and wore again the soft moccasins.

While Dawee was busily preparing to go I controlled my tears. But when I heard him bounding away on his pony, I buried my face in my arms and cried hot tears.

My mother was troubled by my unhappiness. Coming to my side, she offered me the only printed matter we had in our home. It was an Indian Bible, given her some years ago by a missionary. She tried to console me. "Here, my child, are the white man's papers. Read a little from them," she said most piously.

I took it from her hand, for her sake; but my enraged spirit felt more like burning the book, which afforded me no help and was a perfect delusion to my mother. I did not read it but laid it unopened on the floor, where I sat on my feet. The dim yellow light of the braided muslin burning in a small vessel of oil flickered and sizzled in the awful silent storm which followed my rejection of the Bible.

Now my wrath against the fates consumed my tears before they reached my eyes. I sat stony, with a bowed head. My mother threw a shawl over her head and shoulders and stepped out into the night.

After an uncertain solitude, I was suddenly aroused by a loud *cry* piercing the night. It was my mother's voice wailing among the barren hills which held the bones of buried warriors. She called aloud for her brothers' spirits to support her in her helpless misery. My fingers grew icy cold, as I realized that my unrestrained tears had betrayed my suffering to her, and she was grieving for me.

Before she returned, though I knew she was on her way, for she had ceased her weeping, I extinguished the light and leaned my head on the window sill.

Many schemes of running away from my surroundings hovered about in my mind. A few more moons of such a turmoil drove me away to the Eastern school. I rode on the white man's iron steed, thinking it would bring me back to my mother in a few winters, when I should be grown tall and there would be congenial friends awaiting me.

VII. Incurring My Mother's Displeasure

In the second journey to the East I had not come without some precautions. I had a secret interview with one of our best medicine men, and when I left his wigwam I carried securely in my sleeve a tiny bunch of magic roots. This possession assured me of friends wherever I should go. So absolutely did I believe in its charms that I wore it through all the school routine for more than a year. Then, before I lost my faith in the dead roots, I lost the little buckskin bag containing all my good luck.

At the close of this second term of three years I was the proud owner of my first diploma. The following autumn I ventured upon a college career against my mother's will.

I had written for her approval, but in her reply I found no encouragement. She called my notice to her neighbors' children, who had completed their education in three years. They had returned to their homes and were then talking English with the frontier settlers. Her few words hinted that I had better give up my slow attempt to learn the white man's ways and be content to roam over the prairies and find my living upon wild roots. I silenced her by deliberate disobedience.

Thus, homeless and heavy-hearted, I began anew my life among strangers.

As I hid myself in my little room in the college dormitory, away from the scornful and yet curious eyes of the students, I pined for sympathy. Often I wept in secret, wishing I had gone West, to be nourished by my mother's love, instead of remaining among a cold race whose hearts were frozen hard with prejudice.

During the fall and winter seasons I scarcely had a real friend, though by that time several of my classmates were courteous to me at a safe distance.

My mother had not yet forgiven my rudeness to her, and I had no moment for letter-writing. By daylight and lamplight, I spun with reeds and thistles until my hands were tired from their weaving the magic design which promised me the white man's respect.

At length, in the spring term, I entered an oratorical contest among the various classes. As the day of competition approached, it did not seem possible that the event was so near at hand, but it came. In the chapel the classes assembled together with their invited guests. The high platform was carpeted and gayly festooned with college colors. A bright white light illumined the room and outlined clearly the great polished beams that arched the domed ceiling. The assembled crowds filled the air with pulsating murmurs. When the hour for speaking arrived all were hushed. But on the wall the old clock which pointed out the trying moment ticked calmly on.

One after another I saw and heard the orators. Still, I could not realize that they longed for the favorable decision of the judges as much as I did. Each contestant received a loud burst of applause, and some were cheered heartily. Too soon my turn came, and I paused a moment behind the curtains for a deep breath. After my concluding words, I heard the same applause that the others had called out.

Upon my retreating steps, I was astounded to receive from my fellow students a large bouquet of roses tied with flowing ribbons. With the lovely flowers I fled from the stage. This friendly token was a rebuke to me for the hard feelings I had borne them.

Later, the decision of the judges awarded me the first place. Then there was a mad uproar in the hall, where my classmates sang and shouted my name at the top of their lungs and the disappointed students howled and brayed in fearfully dissonant tin trumpets. In this excitement, happy students rushed forward to offer their congratulations. And I could not conceal a smile when they wished to escort me in a procession to the students' parlor, where all were going to calm themselves. Thanking them for the kind spirit which prompted them to make such a proposition, I walked alone in the night to my own little room.

A few weeks afterward, I appeared as the college representative in another contest. This time the competition was among orators from different colleges in our state. It was held at the state capital in one of the largest opera houses.

Here again was a strong prejudice against my people. In the evening, as the great audience filled the house, the student bodies began warring among themselves. Fortunately, I was spared witnessing any of the noisy wrangling before the contest began. The slurs against the Indian that stained the lips of our opponents were already burning like a dry fever within my breast.

But after the orations were delivered a deeper burn awaited me. There, before that vast ocean of eyes, some college rowdies threw out a large white flag, with a drawing of a most forlorn Indian girl on it. Under this they had printed in bold black letters words that ridiculed the college which was represented by a "squaw." Such worse than barbarian rudeness embittered me. While we waited for the verdict of the judges, I gleamed fiercely upon the throngs of palefaces. My teeth were hard set, as I saw the white flag still floating insolently in the air.

Then anxiously we watched the man carry toward the stage the envelope containing the final decision.

There were two prizes given that night, and one of them was mine!

The evil spirit laughed within me when the white flag dropped out of sight and the hands which furled it hung limp in defeat.

Leaving the crowd as quickly as possible, I was soon in my room. The rest of the night I sat in an armchair and gazed into the crackling fire. I laughed no more in triumph when thus alone. The little taste of victory did not satisfy a hunger in my heart. In my mind I saw my mother far away on the Western plains, and she was holding a charge against me.

An Indian Teacher Among Indians

by Zitkala-Sa

I. My First Day

Though an illness left me unable to continue my college course, my pride kept me from returning to my mother. Had she known of my worn condition, she would have said the white man's papers were not worth the freedom and health I had lost by them. Such a rebuke from my mother would have been unbearable, and as I felt then, it would be far too true to be comfortable.

Since the winter when I had my first dreams about red apples I had been traveling slowly toward the morning horizon. There had been no doubt about the direction in which I wished to go to spend my energies in a work for the Indian race. Thus I had written my mother briefly, saying my plan for the year was to teach in an Eastern Indian school. Sending this message to her in the West, I started at once eastward.

Thus I found myself, tired and hot, in a black veiling of car smoke, as I stood wearily on a street corner of an old-fashioned town, waiting for a car. In a few moments more I should be on the school grounds, where a new work was ready for my inexperienced hands.

Upon entering the school campus, I was surprised at the thickly clustered buildings which made it a quaint little village, much more interesting than the town itself. The large trees among the houses gave the place a cool, refreshing shade and the grass a deeper green. Within this large court of grass and trees stood a low green pump. The queer boxlike case had a revolving handle on its side, which clanked and creaked constantly.

I made myself known and was shown to my room—a small, carpeted room, with ghastly walls and ceiling. The two windows, both on the same side, were curtained with heavy muslin yellowed with age. A clean white bed was in one corner of the room, and opposite it was a square pine table covered with a black woolen blanket.

Without removing my hat from my head, I seated myself in one of the two stiff-backed chairs that were placed beside the table. For several heart throbs I sat still, looking from ceiling to floor, from wall to wall, trying hard to imagine years of contentment there. Even while I was wondering if my exhausted strength would sustain me through this undertaking, I heard a heavy hand knock at my door. Opening it, I met the imposing figure of a stately gray-haired man. With a light straw hat in one hand and the right hand extended for greeting, he smiled kindly upon me. For some reason I was awed by his wondrous height and his strong square shoulders, which I felt were a finger's length above my head.

I was always slight, and my serious illness in the early spring had made me look rather frail and languid. His quick eye measured my height and breadth. Then he looked into my face. I imagined that a visible shadow flitted across his countenance as he let my hand fall. I knew he was no other than my employer.

"Ah ha! so you are the little Indian girl who created the excitement among the college orators!" he said, more to himself than to me. I thought I heard a subtle note of disappointment in his voice. Looking in from where he stood, with one sweeping glance, he asked if I lacked anything for my room.

After he turned to go, I listened to his step until it grew faint and was lost in the distance. I was aware that my car-smoked appearance had not concealed the lines of pain on my face.

For a short moment my spirit laughed at my ill fortune, and I entertained the idea of exerting myself to make an improvement. But as I tossed my hat off, a leaden weakness came over me, and I felt as if years of weariness lay like water-soaked logs upon me. I threw myself upon the bed and, closing my eyes, forgot my good intention.

II. A Trip Westward

One sultry month I sat at a desk heaped up with work. Now, as I recall it, I wonder how I could have dared to disregard nature's warning with such recklessness. Fortunately, my inheritance of a marvelous endurance enabled me to bend without breaking.

Though I had gone to and fro, from my room to the office, in an unhappy silence, I was watched by those around me. On an early morning I was summoned to the superintendent's office. For a half hour I listened to his words, and when I returned to my room I remembered one sentence above the rest. It was this: "I am going to turn you loose to pasture!" He was sending me West to gather Indian pupils for the school, and this was his way of expressing it.

I needed nourishment, but the midsummer's travel across the continent to search the hot prairies for overconfident parents who would entrust their children to strangers was a lean pasturage. However, I dwelt on the hope of seeing my mother. I tried to reason that a change was a rest. Within a couple of days I started toward my mother's home.

The intense heat and the sticky car smoke that followed my homeward trail did not noticeably restore my vitality. Hour after hour I gazed upon the country which was receding rapidly from me. I noticed the gradual expansion of the horizon as we emerged out of the forests into the plains. The great high buildings, whose towers overlooked the dense woodlands and whose gigantic clusters formed large cities, diminished, together with the groves, until only little log cabins lay snugly in the bosom of the vast prairie. The cloud shadows which drifted about on the waving yellow long-dried grasses thrilled me like the meeting of old friends.

At a small station, consisting of a single frame house with a rickety boardwalk around it, I alighted from the iron horse just thirty miles from my mother and my brother Dawee. A strong hot wind seemed determined to blow my hat off and return me to olden days when I roamed bareheaded over the hills. After the puffing engine of my train was gone, I stood on the platform in deep solitude. In the distance I saw the gently rolling land leap up into bare hills. At their bases a broad gray road was winding itself round about them until it came by the station. Among these hills I rode in a light conveyance, with a trusty driver, whose unkempt flaxen hair hung shaggy about his ears and his leather neck of reddish tan. From accident or decay he had lost one of his long front teeth.

Though I call him a paleface, his cheeks were of a brick red. His moist blue eyes, blurred and bloodshot, twitched involuntarily. For a long time he had driven through grass and snow from this solitary station to the Indian village. His weather-stained clothes fitted badly his warped shoulders. He was stooped, and his protruding chin, with its tuft of dry flax, nodded as monotonously as did the head of his faithful beast.

All the morning I looked about me, recognizing old familiar skylines of rugged bluffs and round-topped hills. By the roadside I caught glimpses of various plants whose sweet roots were delicacies among my people. When I saw the first cone-shaped wigwam, I could not help uttering an exclamation which caused my driver a sudden jump out of his drowsy nodding.

At noon, as we drove through the eastern edge of the reservation, I grew very impatient and restless. Constantly I wondered what my mother would say upon seeing her little daughter grown tall. I had not written her the day of my arrival, thinking I would surprise her. Crossing a ravine thicketed with low shrubs and plum bushes, we approached a large yellow acre of wild sunflowers. Just beyond this nature's garden we drew near to my mother's cottage. Close by the log cabin stood a little canvas-covered wigwam. The driver stopped in front of the open door, and in a long moment my mother appeared at the threshold.

I had expected her to run out to greet me, but she stood still, all the while staring at the weather-beaten man at my side. At length, when her loftiness became unbearable, I called to her, "Mother, why do you stop?"

This seemed to break the evil moment, and she hastened out to hold my head against her cheek.

"My daughter, what madness possessed you to bring home such a fellow?" she asked, pointing at the driver, who was fumbling in his pockets for change while he held the bill I gave him between his jagged teeth.

"Bring him! Why, no, mother, he has brought me!" I exclaimed.

Upon this revelation, my mother threw her arms about me and apologized for her mistaken inference. We laughed away the momentary hurt. Then she built a brisk fire on the ground in the tepee and hung a blackened coffeepot on one of the prongs of a forked pole which leaned over the flames. Placing a pan on a heap of red embers, she baked some unleavened bread. This light luncheon she brought into the cabin and arranged on a table covered with a checkered oilcloth.

My mother had never gone to school, and though she meant always to give up her own customs for such of the white man's ways as pleased her, she made only compromises. Her two windows, directly opposite each other, she curtained with a pink-flowered print. The naked logs were unstained, and rudely carved with the axe so as to fit into one another. The sod roof was trying to boast of tiny sunflowers, the seeds of which had probably been planted by the constant wind. As I leaned my head against the logs, I discovered the peculiar odor that I could not forget. The rains had soaked the earth and roof so that the smell of damp clay was but the natural breath of such a dwelling.

"Mother, why is not your house cemented? Do you have no interest in a more comfortable shelter?" I asked, when the apparent inconveniences of her home seemed to suggest indifference on her part.

"You forget, my child, that I am now old, and I do not work with beads any more. Your brother Dawee, too, has lost his position, and we are left without means to buy even a morsel of food," she replied.

Dawee was a government clerk on our reservation when I last heard from him. I was surprised upon hearing what my mother said concerning his lack of employment. Seeing the puzzled expression on my face, she continued "Dawee! Oh, has he not told you that the Great Father at Washington sent a white son to take your brother's pen from him? Since then Dawee has not been able to make use of the education the Eastern school has given him "

I found no words with which to answer satisfactorily. I found no reason with which to cool my inflamed feelings.

Dawee was a whole day's journey off on the prairie, and my mother did not expect him until the next day. We were silent.

When, at length, I raised my head to hear more clearly the moaning of the wind in the corner logs, I noticed the daylight streaming into the dingy room through several places where the logs tatted unevenly. Turning to my mother I urged her to tell me more about Dawee's trouble, but she only said: "Well, my daughter, this village has been these many winters a refuge for white robbers. The Indian cannot complain to the Great Father in Washington without suffering outrage for it here. Dawee tried to secure justice for our tribe in a small matter, and today you see the folly of it."

Again, though she stopped to hear what I might say, I was silent.

"My child, there is only one source of justice, and I have been praying steadfastly to the Great Spirit to avenge our wrongs," she said, seeing I did not move my lips.

My shattered energy was unable to hold longer any faith, and I cried out desperately: "Mother, don't pray again! The Great Spirit does not care if we live or die! Let us not look for good or justice: then we shall not be disappointed!"

"Ssh! my child, do not talk so madly. There is Taku Iyotan Wasaka, to which I pray," she answered, as she stroked my head again as she used to do when I was a smaller child.

III. My Mother's Curse Upon White Settlers

One black night mother and I sat alone in the dim starlight in front of our wigwam. We were facing the river, as we talked about the shrinking limits of the village. She told me about the poverty-stricken white settlers, who lived in caves dug in the long ravines of the high hills across the river.

A whole tribe of broad-footed white beggars had rushed hither to make claims on those wild lands. Even as she was telling this I spied a small glimmering light in the bluffs.

"That is a white man's lodge where you see the burning fire," she said. Then, a short distance from it, only a little lower than the first, was another light. As I became accustomed to the night, I saw more and more twinkling lights, here and there, scattered all along the wide black margin of the river.

Still looking toward the distant firelight, my mother continued, "My daughter, beware of the paleface. It was the cruel paleface who caused the death of your sister and your uncle, my brave brother. It is this same paleface who offers in one palm the holy papers, and with the other gives a holy baptism of firewater. He is the hypocrite who reads with one eye, 'Thou shalt not kill,' and with the other gloats upon the sufferings of the Indian race." Then suddenly discovering a new fire in the bluffs, she exclaimed, "Well, well, my daughter, there is the light of another white rascal!"

She sprang to her feet, and, standing firm beside her wigwam, she sent a curse upon those who sat around the hated white man's light. Raising her right arm forcibly into line with her eye, she threw her whole might into her doubled fist as she shot it vehemently at the strangers. Long she held her outstretched fingers toward the settler's lodge, as if an invisible power passed from them to the evil at which she aimed.

IV. Retrospection

Leaving my mother, I returned to the school in the East. As months passed over me, I slowly comprehended that the large army of white teachers in Indian schools had a larger missionary creed than I had suspected.

It was one which included self-preservation quite as much as Indian education. When I saw an opium- eater holding a position as teacher of Indians, I did not understand what good was expected, until a Christian in power replied that this pumpkin-colored creature had a feeble mother to support. An inebriate paleface sat stupid in a doctor's chair, while Indian patients carried their ailments to untimely graves, because his fair wife was dependent upon him for her daily food.

I find it hard to count that white man a teacher who tortured an ambitious Indian youth by frequently reminding the brave changeling that he was nothing but a "government pauper."

Though I burned with indignation upon discovering on every side instances no less shameful than those I have mentioned, there was no present help. Even the few rare ones who have worked nobly for my race were powerless to choose work-men like themselves. To be sure, a man was sent from the Great Father to inspect

Indian schools, but what he saw was usually the students' sample work *made* for exhibition. I was nettled by this sly cunning of the workmen who hoodwinked the Indian's pale Father at Washington.

My illness, which prevented the conclusion of my college course, together with my mother's stories of the encroaching frontier settlers, left me in no mood to strain my eyes in searching for latent good in my white co-workers.

At this stage of my own evolution, I was ready to curse men of small capacity for being the dwarfs their God had made them. In the process of my education I had lost all consciousness of the nature world about me. Thus, when a hidden rage took me to the small white-walled prison which I then called my room, I unknowingly turned away from my one salvation.

Alone in my room, I sat like the petrified Indian woman of whom my mother used to tell me. I wished my heart's burdens would turn me to unfeeling stone. But alive, in my tomb, I was destitute!

For the white man's papers I had given up my faith in the Great Spirit. For these same papers I had forgotten the healing in trees and brooks. On account of my mother's simple view of life, and my lack of any, I gave her up also. I made no friends among the race of people I loathed. Like a slender tree, I had been uprooted from my mother, nature, and God. I was shorn of my branches, which had waved in sympathy and love for home and friends. The natural coat of bark which had protected my oversensitive nature was scraped off to the very quick.

Now a cold bare pole I seemed to be, planted in a strange earth. Still, I seemed to hope a day would come when my mute aching head, reared upward to the sky, would flash a zigzag lightning across the heavens. With this dream of vent for a long-pent consciousness, I walked again amid the crowds.

At last, one weary day in the schoolroom, a new idea presented itself to me. It was a new way of solving the problem of my inner self. I liked it. Thus I resigned my position as teacher, and now I am in an Eastern city, following the long course of study I have set for myself. Now, as I look back upon the recent past, I see it from a distance, as a whole. I remember how, from morning till evening, many specimens of civilized peoples visited the Indian school. The city folks with canes and eyeglasses, the countrymen with sunburnt cheeks and clumsy feet, forgot their relative social ranks in an ignorant curiosity. Both sorts of these Christian palefaces were alike astounded at seeing the children of savage warriors so docile and industrious.

An Unquiet Mind

by Kay Redfield Jamison

College, for many people I know, was the best time of their lives. This is inconceivable to me. College was, for the most part, a terrible struggle, a recurring nightmare of violent and dreadful moods spelled only now and again by weeks, sometimes months, of great fun, passion, high enthusiasms, and long runs of very hard but enjoyable work. This pattern of shifting moods and energies had a very seductive side to it, in large part because of fitful reinfusions of the intoxicating moods that I had enjoyed in high school. These were quite extraordinary, filling my brain with a cataract of ideas and more than enough energy to give me at least the illusion of carrying them out. My normal Brooks Brothers conservatism would go by the board; my hemlines would go up, my neckline down, and I would enjoy the sensuality of my youth. Almost everything was done to excess: instead of buying one Beethoven symphony I would buy nine; instead of enrolling for five classes I would enroll in seven; instead of buying two tickets for a concert I would buy eight or ten.

One day, during my freshman year, I was walking through the botanical gardens at UCLA, and, gazing down into the small brook that flows through the gardens, I suddenly and powerfully was reminded of a scene from Tennyson's *Idylls of the King*. Something, I think, about the Lady of the Lake. Compelled with an immediate and inflaming sense of urgency, I ran off to the bookstore to track down a copy of it, which I did. By the time I left the student union I was weighed down with at least twenty other books, some of which were related to Tennyson's poem but others of which were only very tangentially connected, if at all, to the Arthurian legend: Malory's *Le Morte d'Arthur* and T. H. White's *The Once and Future King* were added, as were *The Golden Bough, The Celtic Realm, The Letters of Heloise and Abelard,* books by Jung, books by Robert Graves, books about Tristan and Isolde, anthologies of creation myths, and collections of Scottish fairy tales. They all seemed very related to one another at the time. Not only did they seem related, but they seemed together to contain some essential key to the grandiosely tizzied view of the universe that my mind was beginning to spin. The Arthurian tragedy explained everything there was to know about human nature—its passions, betrayals, violence, grace, and aspirations—and my mind wove and wove, propelled by the certainty of absolute truth. Naturally, given the universality of my insights, these purchases seemed absolutely essential at the time. Indeed, they had a certain rapturous logic to them. But in the world of more prosaic realities, I could ill afford the kind of impulsive buying that this represented. I was working twenty to thirty hours a week in order to pay my way through college, and there was no margin at all for the expenses I ran up during these times of high enthusiasms. Unfortunately, the pink overdraft notices from my bank always seemed to arrive when I was in the throes of the depression that inevitably followed my weeks of exaltation.

Much as it had during my senior year in high school, my classwork during these galvanized periods seemed very straightforward, and I found examinations, laboratory work, and papers almost absurdly easy during the weeks that the high-flying times would last. I also would become immersed in a variety of political and social causes that included everything from campus antiwar activities to slightly more idiosyncratic zealotries, such as protesting cosmetic firms that killed turtles in order to manufacture and sell beauty products. At one point I picketed a local department store with a homemade placard that showed two very badly drawn sea turtles scrunching their way across the sand, with bits of starlight overhead—a crushing reminder, I thought, of their remarkable navigational abilities—and the words YOUR SKIN HAS COST THEM THEIRS printed in large red letters beneath the picture.

But then as night inevitably goes after the day, my mood would crash, and my mind again would grind to a halt. I lost all interest in my schoolwork, friends, reading, wandering, or daydreaming. I had no idea of what was happening to me, and I would wake up in the morning with a profound sense of dread that I was going to have to somehow make it through another entire day. I would sit for hour after hour in the undergraduate library, unable to muster up enough energy to go to class. I would stare out the window, stare at my books, rearrange them, shuffle them around, leave them unopened, and think about dropping out of college. When I did go to class it was pointless. Pointless and painful. I understood very little of what was going on, and I felt as though only dying would release me from the overwhelming sense of inadequacy and blackness that surrounded me. I felt utterly alone, and watching the animated conversations between my fellow students only made me feel more so. I stopped answering the telephone and took endless hot baths in the vain hope that I might somehow escape from the deadness and dreariness.

On occasion, these periods of total despair would be made even worse by terrible agitation. My mind would race from subject to subject, but instead of being filled with the exuberant and cosmic thoughts that had been associated with earlier periods of rapid thinking, it would be drenched in awful sounds and images of decay and dying: dead bodies on the beach, charred remains of animals, toe-tagged corpses in morgues. During these agitated periods I became exceedingly restless, angry, and irritable, and the only way I could dilute the agitation was to run along the beach or pace back and forth across my room like a polar bear at the zoo. I had no idea what was going on, and I felt totally unable to ask anyone for help. It never occurred to me that I was ill; my brain just didn't put it in those terms. Finally, however, after hearing a lecture about depression in my abnormal psychology course, I went to the student health service with the intention of asking to see a psychiatrist. I got as far as the stairwell just outside the clinic but was only able to sit there, paralyzed with fear and shame, unable to go in and unable to leave. I must have sat there, head in my hands, sobbing, for more than an hour. Then I left and never went back. Eventually, the depression went away of its own accord, but only long enough for it to regroup and mobilize for the next attack.

This Boy's Life

by Tobias Wolff

Dwight drove in a sullen reverie. When I spoke he answered curtly or not at all. Now and then his expression changed, and he grunted as if to claim some point of argument. He kept a Camel burning on his lower lip. Just the other side of Concrete he pulled the car hard to the left and hit a beaver that was crossing the road. Dwight said he had swerved to miss the beaver, but that wasn't true. He had gone out of his way to run over it. He stopped the car on the shoulder of the road and backed up to where the beaver lay.

We got out and looked at it. I saw no blood. The beaver was on its back with its eyes open and its curved yellow teeth bared. Dwight prodded it with his foot. "Dead," he said.

It was dead all right.

"Pick it up," Dwight told me. He opened the trunk of the car and said, "Pick it up. We'll skin the sucker out when we get home."

I wanted to do what Dwight expected me to do, but I couldn't. I stood where I was and stared at the beaver.

Dwight came up beside me. "That pelt's worth fifty dollars, bare minimum." He added, "Don't tell me you're afraid of the damned thing."

"No sir."

"Then pick it up." He watched me. "It's dead, for Christ's sake. It's just meat. Are you afraid of hamburger? Look." He bent down and gripped the tail in one hand and lifted the beaver off the ground. He tried to make this appear effortless but I could see he was surprised and strained by the beaver's weight. A stream of blood ran out of its nose, then stopped. A few drops fell on Dwight's shoes before he jerked the body away. Holding the beaver in front of him with both hands, Dwight carried it to the open trunk and let go. It landed hard. "There," he said, and wiped his hands on his pant leg.

We drove farther into the mountains. It was late after noon. Pale cold light. The river flashed green through the trees beside the road, then turned gray as pewter when the sun dropped. The mountains darkened. Night came on.

Dwight stopped at a tavern in a village called Marblemount, the last settlement before Chinook. He brought a hamburger and fries out to the car and told me to sit tight for a while, then he went back inside. After I finished eating I put my coat on and waited for Dwight. Time passed, and more time. Every so often I got out of the car and walked short distances up and down the road. Once I risked a look through the tavern window but the glass was fogged up. I went back to the car and listened to the radio, keeping a sharp eye on the tavern door. Dwight had told me not to use the radio because it might wear down the battery. I still felt bad about being afraid of the beaver, and I didn't want to get in more trouble. I wanted everything to go just right.

I had agreed to move to Chinook partly because I thought I had no choice. But there was more to it than that. Unlike my mother, I was fiercely conventional. I was tempted by the idea of belonging to a conventional family, and living in a house, and having a big brother and a couple of sisters especially if one of those sisters was Norma. And in my heart I despised the life I led in Seattle. I was sick of it and had no idea how to change it. I thought that in Chinook, away from Taylor and Silver, away from Marian, away from people who had already made up their minds about me, I could be different. I could introduce myself as a scholar-athlete, a boy of dignity and consequence, and without any reason to doubt me people would believe I was that boy, and thus allow me to be that boy. I recognized no obstacle to miraculous change but the incredulity of others. This was an idea that died hard, if it ever really died at all.

I played the radio softly, thinking I'd use less power that way. Dwight came out of the tavern a long time after he went in, at least as long a time as we'd spent getting there from Seattle, and gunned the car out of the lot. He drove fast, but I didn't worry until we hit a long series of curves and the car began to fishtail. This stretch of the road ran alongside a steep gorge; to our right the slope fell almost sheer to the river. Dwight sawed the wheel back and forth, seeming not to hear the scream of the tires. When I reached out for the dashboard he glanced at me and asked what I was afraid of now.

I said I was a little sick to my stomach.

"Sick to your stomach? A hotshot like you?"

The headlights slid off the road into darkness, then back again. "I'm not a hotshot," I said.

"That's what I hear. I hear you're a real hotshot. Come and go where you please, when you please. Isn't that right?"

I shook my head.

"That's what I hear," he said. "Regular man about town. Performer, too. That right? You a performer?"

"No sir."

"That's a goddamned lie." Dwight kept looking back and forth between me and the road.

"Dwight, please slow down," I said.

"If there's one thing I can't stomach," Dwight said, "it's a liar."

I pushed myself against the seat. "I'm not a liar."

"Sure you are. You or Marian. Is Marian a liar?"

I didn't answer.

"She says you're quite the little performer. Is that a lie? You tell me that's a lie and we'll drive back to Seattle so you can call her a liar to her face. You want me to do that?"

I said no, I didn't.

"Then you must be the one that's the liar. Right?"

I nodded.

"Marian says you're quite the little performer. Is that true?"

"I guess," I said.

"You guess. You *guess*. Well, let's see your act. Go on. Let's see your act." When I didn't do anything, he said, "I'm waiting."

"I can't."

"Sure you can."

"No sir."

"Sure you can. Do me. I hear you do me."

I shook my head.

"Do me, I hear you're good at doing me. Do me with the lighter. Here. Do me with the lighter." He held out the Zippo in its velvet case. "Go on."

I sat where I was, both hands on the dashboard. We were all over the road.

"Take it!"

I didn't move.

He put the lighter back in his pocket. "Hotshot," he said. "You pull that hotshot stuff around me and I'll snatch you bald-headed, you understand?"

"Yes sir."

"You're in for a change, mister. You got that? You're in for a whole 'nother ball game."

I braced myself for the next curve.

Young and Disabled

by Nancy Mairs

LUNCHTIME. Your favorite cafe. Blinking away the dust and glare of the street, your gaze falls on a woman at the corner table. Her dark hair swings softly against cheeks as flawless as porcelain, and her chin rests on the slender fingers of one hand. In her beige silk blouse and ivory linen suit, she has the crisp appearance of someone who holds a powerful job and does it well. She leans forward to say something to the man across from her, and when he throws his head back with a deep laugh, her eyes sparkle.

Yourself, you're having a bad-hair day, and a zing up your calf tells you you're going to have to dash into the drugstore for a new pair of pantyhose before returning to your office, where the world's most boring report lies on your desk, still only half read. You stayed awake half the night worrying whether your boyfriend will take the job he's been offered in Denver, and now your brain feels as soggy as a fallen log under a thick layer of moss. But your stomach is rumbling, so you head for a table in the back.

As you pass the woman, you see with a start that she's sitting in a wheelchair. "Oh, the poor thing!" you think. "How courageous she is to fix herself up and get out of the house on a day as hot as this. And what a thoughtful man—her brother, it must be—treating her to lunch to cheer her up." In an instant, your mossy brain has dredged up an entirely new creature. The person you first noticed—the glamorous career woman enjoying a flirtation over lunch—is no more real, of course, than this pitiful invalid putting a brave face on her misery. Both are projections of your own imagination—your desires, your dreads. But because you admire the first, you're more likely to want to know her; the second, because she makes you uneasy, will remain a stranger.

The "you" I refer to is as much my young self as she is anyone else. In those days, I knew almost no one with a disability. When I was a child, one of my uncles had become partially paralyzed by polio, but he moved to Florida and I seldom saw him after that. Although two of my college classmates had been disabled, one quite severely, and I remember watching in wonder as she maneuvered her crutches over paths made treacherous by the New England winter, I didn't happen to know—or did I avoid knowing?—either of them well. Those were the days before buildings were ramped, elevators installed, and bathrooms modified for accessibility, and I can't imagine how complicated and exhausting and downright dangerous their lives must have been. No wonder relatively few disabled people ventured out into the world.

Then I became one of them. When my neurologist diagnosed my multiple sclerosis, he told me that I had a "normal" life expectancy. But, he didn't have to tell me, I wouldn't have a "normal" life, not the one I had prepared myself to live. I was going to be "disabled," more severely as time went on, and I had no idea how to live such a life. Could I go on teaching, and if so, would anybody want to hire me? Would my husband still find me sexually attractive, and could he accept my increasing need for help? Would my children resent having a mother who couldn't do everything that other mothers could? How would I survive if they all abandoned me? Did I even want to live to find out the answers to these questions?

As such questions suggest, I subscribed to the major social myths about the "disabled woman": that she lacks the health or competence to hold a job; that no man could want her or care for her, either physically or emotionally; that disability can only damage, never enhance, friendships and family relationships; that suicide is an understandable, even a rational, response to physical impairment, rather than the symptom of depression it is known to be in nondisabled people. Above all, I felt permanently exiled from "normality." Whether imposed by self or society, this outsider status—and not the disability itself—constitutes the most daunting barrier for most people with physical impairments, because it, even more than flights of steps or elevators without braille, prevents them from participating fully in the ordinary world, where most of life's satisfactions dwell.

Gradually, I stopped thinking of myself as an outcast, and over the years I have watched the social barriers crumbling as well. As technological advances permit disabled people to travel, study, and work, and as the media incorporate their pictures and stories into articles, advertising, television programs, and films, their presence becomes more familiar and less frightening. Many of them are eager to promote this process, as *Glamour* magazine discovered by asking readers with disabilities to write about their histories and the effects that their physical circumstances have had on their work, their friendships, and their love lives. Letters and faxes flooded in from several hundred women (and a handful of men), ranging in age from sixteen to eighty-five but most in their twenties and thirties, who were "intrigued," "excited," and "thrilled" at being asked to emerge from the shadows. Having the chance to collate these for an article I wrote for the magazine, I became charmed by the frankness, grit, and good humor these women displayed.

The challenge in compressing their replies—many of them covering several closely typed or handwritten pages—lay in fairly representing their diversity. Their disabilities varied so widely that it was difficult—even deceptive—to generalize about such women, who may have less in common with each other than they do with some nondisabled women and who may even be made uneasy by women with disabilities different from their own. As Peggy Merriman, who was diagnosed with multiple sclerosis when she was nineteen, protested, "The general public seems to have an easier time (or simply unconsciously prefers) dealing with people with disabilities by lumping us all together and assuming that we all have the same problems and, what is worse, that *all* we deal with or have in our life is our disability." But defining someone solely in terms of what she cannot do tends to distort her life: "I feel I have been neatly tucked into a category with no room to move," wrote twenty-one-year-old Naomi Passman, whose legs were paralyzed in infancy by a spinal tumor, but "the last thing I need are limits!" I hope that, as these women speak, "disability" will emerge as one element of their complicated personalities and not as a confining category.

Nevertheless, as every woman who wrote to *Glamour* has long since found out, breaking free of a category doesn't abolish the realities of the disability itself, which may include weakness, fatigue, deformity, physical pain, bouts of illness, and reliance on technical assistance like crutches, wheelchairs, or hearing aids. In a society that equates "vitality" and "beauty" with physical soundness, a disabled woman must come to terms with serious shortcomings often earlier and even more urgently than others. In this process, these women have learned from experience what many their age understand only intellectually, that life itself is imperfect: the best qualified person doesn't always get the job, the most loving heart doesn't always find a mate. Although a few responded to such knowledge with bitterness or apathy, most seemed to take it as a challenge. Their lives might not be "perfect" by conventional social standards, but they were determined to live productively and passionately anyway.

Those who were disabled from birth, by conditions like spine bifida and cerebral palsy, had to cope with being "different" during the time when social conformity seems most compelling. For many of them, childhood was anything but carefree, since they often faced both painful medical treatments and the taunts of "normal" schoolmates. Their reactions to their situations often diverged, however, as revealed by the responses of two women with osteogenesis imperfecta, a genetic disorder that causes bones to fracture very easily. "My parents were somewhat over-protective, which is highly understandable," wrote Felicia Wells Williams, a young African American woman who was born with several ribs and both arms already broken. "However, some of their apprehensiveness about my 'fragile' condition rubbed off on me. As a young child, I was told to be careful and think of the consequences of my actions. So I became fearful of certain things—heights, falling down stairs, etc. I spent a lot of my childhood being a spectator—watching others have fun." Konie Gardner, with the same diagnosis, recalled that her parents assigned her Saturday chores just like her five brothers and sisters and gave her every opportunity to try whatever she wanted. "I was always an accepted kid in the neighborhood, too, and even though I could not physically participate in many of the games, etc., I was an enthusiastic spectator and never felt left out by anyone." Whereas one felt she was missing the fun, the other had fun watching.

Many received the kind of encouragement Kim Silvey reported: born with dislocated hips that required ten operations while she was growing up, Kim "wasn't one to hide and not be seen by anybody," thanks to her parents, who "instilled in me confidence and the belief that I could do anything I wanted, and that's the attitude I grew up with and the one I still hold today." She added, "It would have been so easy for them to coddle me and try to keep me out of the 'evil eye' of the world and to try to shelter me from the pain others could inflict upon me. I credit my being who I am today to my parents' unwillingness to hide me because I didn't fit the 'normal' mold."

Even those with supportive parents often found other children cruel. "With a toe-first walking style, slurred speech and nearly no fine motor coordination, I was not what anyone considered popular," recalled Barbara McGuire, thirty-four, born with cerebral palsy and educated in regular classes. "I was the first to get 'cooties' (call me if you don't remember this social disease of elementary school kids); the last to get rid of them; the first to get teased; the last to get picked in gym." From early on, "boys were terribly mean," and by junior high school girls were, too, "to impress the boys." Only after entering an all-girls' high school did she begin to make lifelong friends.

The struggle for approval from nondisabled peers can have humorous consequences, as Juli Delzer, born with a 60 percent hearing loss in both ears, revealed. "As a child, I was so painfully shy about my deafness that it was embarrassing to let people know that I couldn't hear. I came up with what I call 'deaf answers.' If someone asked me a question that I didn't hear, I would answer with 'yes,' 'no,' or 'I don't know,' hoping that I had covered the bases and given an appropriate answer. This didn't work so well when I moved to a new school. In gym class one day, someone turned around to ask 'What's your name?' To which I answered, 'I don't know.' " Now, planning to do small animal husbandry in the Peace Corps before she begins veterinary school Juli has grown self-assured enough to give up these deaf answers, "but still," she wrote, "I am very aware of my handicap in relationships with men. They can't whisper sweet nothings in my ear because I would be forced to look at them and whisper back, 'What?' "

In addition to a sense of humor, pride did much to carry these women through their awkward childhood years. "On the day I received my first hearing aid, when I was nine years old, my doctor assured me my long hair would easily hide it," wrote Madeline Cohen, a student at Stanford Law School who was also born deaf. "In response, I pulled my hair into a pony tail and walked out of his office with my nose in the air."

The dependencies of childhood—for nurture, instruction, and approval from adults—were often especially hard for these women to outgrow, though virtually all of them appear to have succeeded. The transition was not always a happy one. "As a child I was very much treated like a cossetted princess: dressed in beautiful clothes and sheltered from the outside world," wrote thirty-two-year-old Karyna Laroche, whose muscular dystrophy requires her to rely on caregivers for virtually all her needs. An outstanding student, she attended a special school for disabled students until, at thirteen, she transferred to a regular high school, where "I finally realized just how different I was from other kids, how being disabled was only considered cute and socially acceptable when one is young, otherwise it is a social embarrassment." The shock was so great that, despite outward success, "inwardly I only wanted to die. My first suicide attempt occurred at the age of 16 and suicide plans and attempts continued until I turned 30." Only then did she discover "just how lucky I was to be living on my own (which I love), to have great friends, and to have the chance to build a life based on my needs rather than on others' expectations of me."

More often, simply entering adulthood brought a new rush of self-confidence. When Michele Anne Hope Micheline, a student at Emory University whose spine bifida, though relatively mild, has necessitated a number of operations on her left foot, developed a severe ulcer on her normal right foot during her freshman year, the doctors wanted to amputate the infected bone. "I realized," she reported, "almost like a slap on my face, that I was old enough to tell them that [surgery] was NOT how I wanted it. I had a right to say no, to get a second opinion. To grasp my life." Finding a doctor in whom she had complete confidence, who was able to save all but half of her big toe, and having her left foot reconstructed, she assumed responsibility for her own well-being. She has come to terms with the fact that she will always have to deal with a disability and that doctors, though useful, "can't give you a perfect foot. They can't give you what God didn't. You have to find a substitute within yourself for what you are lacking."

Some respondents had already reached adulthood when, like me, they developed a disabling disease or else were injured in skiing, motorcycle, automobile, or on-the-job accidents—even, in one case, a tornado. After I learned that I had multiple sclerosis, the transitions I had to make, involving the development of a new sense of who I was and what I was good for, required mourning the loss of the "old me" as I confronted a new one who seemed like a stranger. The active young wife and mother faded: no longer could I run after my young children or dance with their father. When my waistlength hair grew too heavy for my weakening hands to wash and brush, I had to cut it off, and suddenly I felt no longer carefree and sexy but practical and matronly. With degenerative conditions like mine, self-definition may have to be revised in this way again and again as new limitations develop.

For those struck by sudden catastrophe, the need to adjust may have come instantly, but the process itself took time. Muffy Davis was fifteen, training to be an Olympic ski racer, when an accident on the slopes left her paralyzed from mid-chest down. "It always amazed me when people would say, 'I don't know how you do it. I could never do it!' You don't have a choice, you just do it! What most people don't realize is that they would do this also. They see a disabled person and immediately put themselves in that person's shoes. What they don't realize is that disabled person didn't just get to wherever she was right away. It took time and grieving, but slowly day by day she got better, and eventually she was right back to attacking life, like she had been before her disability." After graduating from Stanford and before beginning medical school, Muffy plans to "give myself a shot at ski racing again, this time as a disabled athlete. I don't want to have any regrets when I get older." Thanks to adaptive sports equipment, such a goal is within her reach.

Whether gradually or suddenly, disabilities that occur in adulthood require revisions of identity that can yield fresh insight, as Madeline Cohen, who has a degenerative retinal disease in addition to her 85 to 90 percent hearing loss, discovered during a three-week Outward Bound experience after college graduation. "Had I stumbled over your disability survey announcement a few years ago, I might have continued flipping through the magazine with little more than a passing glance," she wrote, because she did not grow up defining herself as disabled. On Outward Bound, she encountered "a virtual assault of obstacles. Not the least of these was learning to recognize my limitations, voice them to my group members, and accept assistance from those around me. The latter was (and remains) the most difficult." As the days went by, she came to perceive that "everyone in my group carried special needs [one, for instance, was terrified of heights, and Madeline was able to talk him through a scary climb] and that by accepting assistance, I was acknowledging my participation in the cooperative human endeavor. Since that time, I have been learning to define myself as a 'person with a disability.' "

Regardless of when their disabled lives began or what pattern they have followed, all the respondents confronted the same issues in the "cooperative human endeavor" known as life as did their nondisabled peers. "People seem surprised and often patronizing when they find out I have a job and a social life," wrote Peggy Merriman, who works for a nonprofit agency assisting released prisoners, as though disability drained away all the interest taken by normal young women and some of us who are not so young in finding meaningful work and developing personal relationships. On the contrary! Despite the enormous variety of their experiences, virtually all the respondents devoted much of their energy to the issues surrounding career and love.

A number were still undergraduate or graduate students, majoring in a variety of fields from art history to animal physiology. Those who had finished school worked in similarly diverse areas, among them education, management, law, health care, and fashion design. Disability often required them to be both flexible and resourceful. "At first I wanted to become a vet," wrote Naomi Passman, "but saw how much lifting was involved and decided against it." Determined to work with animals, she applied to become an apprentice trainer of assistance dogs, but the director of the school turned her down. "I couldn't believe that a person who provided a service for the disabled would not hire me because I was disabled!" Undaunted, she found another program. "I am an Apprentice Assistance Dog Trainer and an Independent Living Specialist. I LOVE my work," she reported.

Even though the Americans with Disabilities Act is supposed to prevent the kind of rejection Naomi experienced, a few of the respondents had encountered outright bias, including retaliation by employers if they applied for workers' compensation after being injured on the job. Felicia Wells Williams, with a bachelor's degree in social work, started her career as an entry-level receptionist. "Once after observing blatant discrimination, I filed an equal employment opportunity suit with the Defense Contract Administration/Department of Defense," she recounted. "With the help of some knowledgeable friends, I not only won my case, but I was given the higher grade plus back pay." Defending one's rights can be tricky, however, since the nondisabled tend to expect people with disabilities to be unfailingly cheerful and passive, as Felicia has learned: "Some people say I am arrogant but I believe if I were of normal height/not disabled, I would be called 'confident' rather than 'bossy' or 'pushy.' "

More subtle forms of intolerance can make the workplace a chilly one for disabled women. "Because my symptoms tend to be invisible, I haven't experienced any real bias or discrimination" as a policy advisor to an elected official, reported Cece Hughley Noel, who has had multiple sclerosis since 1987. "However, on the days that I need a cane it is very difficult for me emotionally. People who I work with every day fail to recognize me on the street. They tend to avert their eyes from 'cripples' and don't meet my eyes or hear my 'hello.' It can be devastating to win their praise for taking charge of a meeting one day, only to be ignored as a 'gimp' on the street, the next." Dealing with pain and fatigue every day, Cece has found herself being resented as well as ignored: "My co-workers get 'snitty' sometimes when I take a break and lie down in my office or leave early."

In addition, Cece wrote, "I've used up all my vacation and sick leave this year and feel as though my back is up against the wall." Some of the respondents, finding themselves in similar situations, have had to give up their jobs, and their comments revealed that in our work-driven society, where what you "do" determines who you "are," lack of employment can erode one's sense of self-worth (not to mention one's bank account). As Stephanie McCarty, who managed a bookstore for ten years until her MS symptoms forced her to go on Social Security Disability, put it, "I often feel flustered when I am asked what I 'do' for a living (they wouldn't believe what I do just to live) and don't quite know what to say. I take classes in pottery, spend a great deal of time in the library (and doctor's office), keep myself busy on my home computer, and concentrate on staying healthy. But these things all seem pretty benign when I am talking to someone with a 'career.' "

Whether they held paid jobs or not, these women craved social contact, even at the risk of awkward encounters.

Many recognized that what seems to be rudeness on the part of nondisabled people often arises from ignorance and fear, which can be more crippling in their own way than a physical disability, and that the best way to relieve these is through education. Their advice was pragmatic: Treat a disabled person as an intelligent and responsible adult. (If she's not, that's her problem, not yours.) Remember that not all disabilities are apparent before you accuse her of malingering or shout at her for taking a handicapped parking space. NEVER take one of these yourself, even if you'll "only be a minute." If she does have an obvious disability, before rushing to her aid, ask "How may I help?" and then follow her instructions carefully, or you may both wind up in a heap on the floor. If she's in a wheelchair, sit down whenever possible so that you can converse eye-to-eye, not eye-to-navel. Don't ask her any questions more personal than you'd feel comfortable answering yourself; "What's wrong with you?" is probably not one of them. Above all, don't offer her pity. She probably doesn't need it. (And when she does, she can take care of the job herself.)

Many spoke warmly of friends who offer, as one anonymous respondent who was left partially paralyzed by a brain tumor put it, "kindness without conde-scension." Most of these friends were not disabled, although some of the women still in college reported involvement in disabled students' groups, and most accommodated a disability without much fuss. With both her hearing and her vision impaired, Madeline Cohen has found that "the people who know me best are great about things like repeating themselves, steering me through dark bars and parking lots, and understanding when I miss the thread of a large, noisy conversation and say something ridiculously unconnected. My friends are used to seeing me bump into any object lower than hip level, collide with small children, and look around blankly for someone standing directly in front of me; they do as much as possible to help me avoid such mishaps without making me feel inadequate or foolish."

Sometimes thoughtless friends cause pain without meaning to. Maree Larson, an assistant producer for a video production company who has spine bifida, recalled attending a political rally with some friends, all but one of whom "walked up the steps and took their seats in the third row," while her wheelchair required her to stay in the first. "Soon, my friend was persuaded to join the others ('but only for a minute,' she said), and I was left by myself for the remaining 10 minutes before the rally began." Even friends who are sympathetic in one area can be insensitive in another, as Konie Gardner discovered when it came to dating: "I can't begin to count the number of times that well-meaning friends would say to me, 'I'll set you up with . . .' and every time, and I do mean every time, they never once did. I don't think people realize how much a person like me clings to every promise, suggestion, or hint that is made in this regard."

In general, these women found romantic and sexual relationships much more difficult to establish and sustain than simple friendships. A number were troubled by the prevailing social perception of disabled women as incapable of and uninterested in sex: "In this culture people with disabilities are expected to be perpetual children which means that sexual expression would not be appropriate and may be considered perverted," observed Pat Danielson, whose juvenile rheumatoid arthritis was diagnosed when she was four; and twenty-three-year-old Kimberly Mangiafico, who has spinal muscular atrophy, protested that her wheelchair gives most men "the impression that I cannot have sex, which is totally not true. I have a great sexual self-image and I am really comfortable in my own skin." Others recognized internal barriers, like Naomi Passman, who reflected, "I have had boyfriends and even a first love. That part has never been a problem for me; however, when it comes to being sexually involved that's when walls go up. Quite honestly, for me it has not been other people's perceptions that have affected the relationships, it has been my own."

Knowing that they, like nondisabled women, will be judged initially on their appearance, many reported taking great care with their clothes, makeup, and hair. Some were aware of the obvious ironies of this emphasis, like Peggy Merriman, who asked a male friend, "in my most unconcerned and disinterested voice, if he thought any guy would ever want to meet or go out with me or even be seen with me, if I was using a wheelchair" and was told, "I don't think it really matters that you're in a wheelchair, because you're so pretty." "Here I was," she went on, "ashamed and embarrassed, because of my physical body. Here he was, praising me and telling me I had nothing to worry about, because of my physical body. He didn't say, 'It doesn't matter, because you are so interesting and intelligent,' or even 'It doesn't matter, because you have such a cute dog, and anyone who wants to play with him knows you and he are a package deal, unfortunately.' *That is* me; that's who I am."

No matter how pretty or smart a woman may be, or how cute her dog is, "dating and initiating a relationship is difficult though because all of the typical rules never seem to apply when you are in a wheelchair," noted Muffy Davis. "Guys feel that they can really flirt with a girl in a chair but they don't see it as anything serious," since she presumably doesn't expect to be asked out. "Also girls with disabilities can put all the moves on guys and yet the guys will never interpret things the right way." Although she has found that she often has to take the lead, "I really like it when, every once in a while, a guy makes the first move."

Too often, however, he doesn't make any move at all. "I am 27 years old and still a virgin, not that is bad, but only that it is really not by my choice," wrote Kim Silvey. "I had a date to my prom when I was a junior in high school and went out on a couple of 'just friends' dates in college, but that is it." But disability didn't take away her dreams: "I want nothing more in life than to get married and have a soulmate, best friend, and lover for life. As each birthday comes and goes, I feel the reality of such happening getting smaller and smaller, and I feel cheated and angry."

Those who had succeeded in establishing relationships often found them complicated, physically and emotionally, by disability. "I worry about what weird noises my body is making that he can hear and I don't," Juli Delzer confided. And a woman who asked to remain anonymous wrote, "Unfortunately, spine bifida did affect my sexual functioning, and I'm not able to achieve orgasm. While we've been able to have a reasonably satisfying sex life without intercourse, I know it bothers my partner that I'm non-orgasmic. I think he sometimes sees it as his failure. I'm very responsive to foreplay with my breasts and around my neck, but am truthfully disappointed myself not to be able to climax." "Due to numbness, weakness, fatigue, and bladder problems we sometimes have to be creative with our lovemaking," noted Stephanie McCarty. A sense of humor also helps: "Often, in the heat of passion, one of my hearing aids will be pressed against a chest, an arm, or a pillow," creating an electronic squeal, wrote Madeline Cohen. "My line, dating back to junior high school: 'Whoops! That's my parents checking up on me.' "

Sometimes the urgency to find a partner contributed to an unwise choice, leading to grief. At twenty-nine, Frances Wallen was paralyzed from the waist down when an 18-wheeler ran a stop sign and struck her red Mazda RX-7. "Before the accident I'd been dating someone fairly seriously," she recalled. "He was wild and unreliable, but I was crazy about him and our affair was very hot. After the accident he was there for me every day and we talked about marriage. I wanted as much of my life back as possible, and figured that this was my last shot at love with someone who could see me without pity. My new husband didn't pity me—he resented me, and took great pleasure in draining me dry financially. I figured he would settle down eventually, but he didn't. We divorced after a year and a half, and I added a broken heart to my list of all my other broken body parts."

But there were happy stories as well. One respondent's husband had abandoned her and their three small children when she was still only mildly disabled by a childhood bout with polio; later, post-polio syndrome caused increasing pain and fatigue, a limp, and breathing problems. At this point, she became friends with a man at the agency where she worked. "He talked to me and we found common ground in our children and love of music," she recollected. "While out in the field I came back to agency headquarters occasionally, and he'd be there, interested in my latest news. When I was moved back on my medical transfer, last year, our friendship grew. I told him, up front, about the polio and the part it played in my life. We married in April 1994. He is there for me, supportive and encouraging and loving. In his eyes I am beautiful, the fact that I have polio doesn't interfere. Through him, I am learning to do my best without exhausting all my energy to 'measure up.' Through him, I've found self-acceptance, self-pride, and love. I look in the mirror and see *normal*."

Fortunately, this experience was far from unique. As Muffy Davis pointed out, "The phone does ring less often, but the guys who do call and are interested are of a higher quality." She's been with one of them for two and a half years now, and many other respondents reported similar good fortune, finding partners who were perceptive, patient, affectionate, and above all reassuring. One respondent, whose brain tumor left her with partial paralysis, as well as hair loss and weight gain, wrote, "Naturally, I don't feel very sexy any more. Yet my husband has continued to treat me with kindness and tenderness. Because of his accepting attitude, my self-esteem has not plummeted entirely." Barbara Maguire, married with two small sons, reflected on her fear that her cerebral palsy might be a burden to her family: "Perhaps my biggest fear is for my husband to someday find out that I am not worth the struggles we've had. He assures me that he is the lucky one and that I am the one 'putting up' with him." "I presently have someone in my life and he is a sweetheart," wrote twenty-five-year-old Stacey Fujii, whose lupus was diagnosed on her twenty-third birthday. "Although he is a surfer, he will do things with me that do not involve the sun, like going out to dinner, to a movie or for a walk on the beach at night. It was very hard for me at first because I felt as if I were holding him back. I was also very insecure about the person I am now, but he always tells me I am beautiful and incredible for what I had to go through. He takes the best care of me and never says I am different, just special."

Not perfect, perhaps, but both normal and special: just the way every women needs to feel. And aided by parents, teachers, friends, lovers, and/or sheer self-determination, the majority of the women who responded had achieved some sense of their own ordinary yet unique qualities. Like Madeline Cohen, they had gained an insight into the human condition which enabled them to see their disabilities as "simply a part of who I am, just as other people have lost parents, gone through divorces, overcome learning disabilities or major illnesses, pulled themselves out of socioeconomic deprivation, or emigrated from war zones." Surely not all would go as far as Kimberly Mangiafico when she wrote that "if I was suddenly given the chance to be able to walk, I would not take it. My being in a wheelchair is part of who I am." But most would understand the self-acceptance her statement implies.

Overall, the women who chose to reveal themselves to *Glamour* were bright, tough, competent, sometimes angry, often funny, and very self-assured—hardly a whiner in the bunch! Theirs were not, as cancer survivor Pat Wallace put it, "triumph-over-tragedy stories" (though there were plenty of tragedies and some triumphs, too, but adventure stories. Stephanie McCarty echoed the sense I often have of exploring uncharted territory: "I feel I have been sent on a journey. I wasn't given a guidebook, so I'll have to draw my own map." In undertaking to live as full human beings in a world intent on reducing them to a set of dysfunctional limbs and organs, they had grown much more vigorous than their sometimes fragile bodies would suggest. As I read and digested their words, I felt honored to count myself among their number.

Lakota Woman

by Mary Crow Dog

I was a loner, always. I was not interested in dresses, makeup, or perfume, the kinds of things some girls are keen on. I was scared of white people and uneasy in their company, so I did not socialize with them. I could not relate to half-bloods and was afraid that full-bloods would not accept me. I could not share the values my mother lived by. For friends I had only a few girls who were like me and shared my thoughts. I had no place to go, but a great restlessness came over me, an urge to get away, no matter where. Nowhere was better than the place I was in. So I did what many of my friends had already done—I ran away. Barbara, being older, had already set the precedent. A clash with my mother had sent Barb on her way. My mother was, at that time, hard to live with. From her point of view, I guess, we were not easy to get along with either. We didn't have a generation gap, we had a generation Grand Canyon. Mother's values were Puritan. She was uptight. I remember when Barbara was about to have her baby, mom cussed her out. Barb was still in high school and my mother was cursing her, calling her a no-good whore, which really shook my sister up. Barb said, "I'm going to have your grandchild, I thought you'd be happy," but my mother was just terrible, telling Barb that she was not her daughter anymore. My sister lost her baby. She had a miscarriage working in a kitchen detail one morning. They gave her a big, heavy dishpan full of cereal to carry and that caused it right there. She lost the baby. She could not get over mother's attitude.

My other sister, Sandra, when she was going to have her eldest boy, Jeff, my mother did the same thing to her, saying, "What the hell are you trying to do to me? I can't hold up my head among my friends!" She was more concerned about her neighbors' attitude than about us. Barb told her, "Mom, if you don't want us around, if you are ashamed of your own grandchildren, then, okay, we'll leave."

I understood how mom was feeling. She was wrapped up in a different culture altogether. We spoke a different language. Words did not mean to her what they meant to us. I felt sorry for her, but we were hurting each other. After Barbara lost her baby she brooded. It seemed as if in her mind she blamed mother for it, as if mother had willed that baby to die. It was irrational, but it was there all the same. Once mother told us after a particularly emotional confrontation, "If you ever need any help, don't come to me!" Of course she did not mean it. She will stick up for us always, but looking over her shoulder in case her friends should disapprove. To be able to hold up your head among what is called "the right kind of people," that is important to her. She has a home, she has a car. She has TV and curtains at the windows. That's where her head is. She is a good, hardworking woman, but she won't go and find out what is really happening. For instance, a girl who worked with mother told her she couldn't reach Barbara at work by phone. Immediately mom jumped to the conclusion that Barb had quit her job. So when my sister got home, she got on her case right away: "I just don't give a damn about you kids! Quitting your job!" continuing in that vein.

Barb just rang up her boss and handed the phone to mom, let her know from the horse's mouth that she had not quit. Then she told mother: "Next time find out and make sure of the facts before you get on my case like that. And don't be so concerned about jobs. There are more important things in life than punching a time clock."

There was that wall of misunderstanding between my mother and us, and I have to admit I did not help in breaking it down. I had little inclination to join the hang-around-the-fort Indians, so one day I just up and left, without saying good-bye. Joining up with other kids in patched Levi's jackets and chokers, our long hair trailing behind us. We traveled and did not give a damn where to.

One or two kids acted like a magnet. We formed groups. I traveled with ten of those new or sometimes old acquaintances in one car all summer long. We had our bedrolls and cooking utensils, and if we ran out of something the pros among us would go and rip off the food. Rip off whatever we needed. We just drifted from place to place, meeting new people, having a good time. Looking back, a lot was based on drinking and drugs. If you had a lot of dope you were everybody's friend, everybody wanted to know you. If you had a car and good grass, then you were about one of the best guys anybody ever knew.

It took me a while to see the emptiness underneath all this frenzied wandering. I liked pot. Barb was an acid freak. She told me she once dropped eight hits of LSD at a time. "It all depends on your mood, on your state of mind," she told me. "If you have a stable mind, it's going to be good. But if you are in a depressed mood, or your friend isn't going to be able to handle it for you, then everything is distorted and you have a very hard time as that drug shakes you up."

Once Barb took some acid in a girl friend's bedroom. There was a huge flag on the wall upside down. The Stars and Stripes hanging upside down used to be an international signal of distress. It was also the American Indian's sign of distress. The Ghost Dancers used to wrap themselves in upside-down flags, dancing that way, crying for a vision until they fell down in a trance. When they came to, they always said that they had been in another world, the world as it was before the white man came, the prairie covered with herds of buffalo and tipi circles full of people who had been killed long ago. The flags which the dancers wore like blankets did not prevent the soldiers from shooting them down. Barb was lying on the bed and the upside-down flag began to work on her mind. She was watching it and it was just rippling up the wall like waves; the stripes and the stars would fall from the flag onto the floor and would scatter into thousands of sprays of light, exploding all over the room. She told me she did not quite know whether it was an old-fashioned vision or just a caricature of one, but she liked it.

After a while of roaming and dropping acid she felt burned out, her brain empty. She said she got tired of it, just one trip after the other. She was waiting, waiting for something, for a sign, but she did not know what she was waiting for. And like her, all the other roaming Indian kids were waiting, just as the Ghost Dancers had waited for the drumbeat, the message the eagle was to bring. I was waiting, too. In the meantime I kept traveling.

I was not into LSD but smoked a lot of pot. People have the idea that reservations are isolated, that what happens elsewhere does not touch them, but it does. We might not share in all the things America has to offer some of its citizens, but some things got to us, all right. The urban Indians from LA, Rapid City, St. Paul, and Denver brought them to us on their visits. For instance, around 1969 or 1970 many half-grown boys in Rosebud were suddenly sniffing glue. If the ghetto Indians brought the city with them to the reservation, so we runaways dragged the rest and its problems around with us in our bedrolls. Wherever we went we formed tiny reservations.

"You are an interesting subculture," an anthropologist in Chicago told me during that time. I didn't know whether that was an insult or a compliment. We both spoke English but could not understand each other. To him I was an interesting zoological specimen to be filed away someplace; to me he was merely ridiculous. But anthropologists are a story in themselves.

It is hard being forever on the move and not having any money. We supported ourselves by shoplifting, "liberating" a lot of stuff. Many of us became real experts at this game. I was very good at it. We did not think that what we were doing was wrong. On the contrary, ripping off gave us a great deal of satisfaction, moral satisfaction. We were meting out justice in reverse. We had always been stolen from by white shopkeepers and government agents. In the 1880s and '90s a white agent on the reservation had a salary of fifteen hundred dollars a year. From this salary he managed to save within five or six years some fifty thousand dollars to retire. He simply stole the government goods and rations he was supposed to distribute among the Indians. On some reservations people were starving to death waiting for rations which never arrived because they had been stolen. In Minnesota the Sioux died like flies. When they complained to their head agent, he told them to eat grass. This set off the so-called Great Sioux Uprising of the 1860s, during which the Indians killed that agent by stuffing earth and grass down his throat.

Then the peddlers arrived with their horse-drawn wagons full of pins and needles, beads and calico, always with a barrel of Indian whiskey under the seat. In no time the wagons became log-cabin stores, the stores shopping emporiums which, over the years, blossomed into combination supermarkets-cafeterias-tourist traps-Indian antiques shops-craft centers-filling stations. The trading post at Wounded Knee which started with almost nothing was, after one short generation, worth millions of dollars.

It did not take a genius to get rich in this business. There was always only one store in any given area. You got your stuff there or you did not get it at all. Even now, trading posts charge much higher prices than stores in the cities charge for the same articles. The trading posts have no competition. They sell beads to Indian craftworkers at six times the price of what they buy them for in New York and pay the Indian artists in cans of beans, also at a big markup.

They give Indians credit against lease money coming in months later—at outrageous interest rates. I have seen traders take Indian jewelry and old beadwork in pawn for five dollars' worth of food and then sell it for hundreds of dollars to a collector when the Indian owner could not redeem the article within a given time. For this reason we looked upon shoplifting as just getting a little of our own back, like counting coup in the old days by raiding the enemy's camp for horses.

I was built just right for the job. I looked much younger than I really was, and being so small I could pretend that I was a kid looking for her mother. If my friends were hungry and wanted something to eat, they would often send me to steal it. Once, early in the game, I was caught with a package of ham, cheese, bread, and sausages under my sweater. Suddenly there was this white guard grabbing me by the arm: "Come this way, come this way!" He was big and I was scared, shaking like a leaf. He was walking down the aisle ordering me to follow him, looking over his shoulder every two or three seconds to make sure that I was still behind him. Whenever he was not looking at me I threw the stuff back into the bins as I was passing them. Just threw them to both sides. So when I finally got to the back they searched me and found nothing. I said: "You goddamn redneck. Just because I'm an Indian you are doing this to me. I'm going to sue you people for slander, for making a false arrest." They had to apologize, telling me it had been a case of mistaken identity. I was fifteen at the time.

There was a further reason for our shoplifting. The store owners provoked it. They expected us to steal. Being Indian, if you went into a store, the proprietor or salesperson would watch you like a hawk. They'd stand next to you, two feet away, with their arms crossed, watching, watching. They didn't do that with white customers.

If you took a little time choosing an item they'd be at your elbow at once hovering over you, asking, "May I help you?" Helping you was the furthest from their mind.

I'd say, "No, I'm just looking." Then if they kept standing there, breathing down my neck, I'd say, "Hey, do you want something from me?" And they answer, "No, just watching."

"Watching what? You think I'm gonna steal something?"

"No. Just watching."

"Well, don't stare at me." But still they were standing there, following every move you made. By then the white customers would be staring, too. I didn't mind, because I and the store owners were in an open, undeclared war, a war at first sight. But they treated even elderly, white-haired, and very respectable Indians the same way. In such situations even the most honest, law-abiding person will experience a mighty urge to pocket some article or other right under their noses. I knew a young teacher, a college graduate, who showed me a carton of cigarettes and a package of Tampax with that incredulous look on her face, saying, "Imagine, I stole this! I can't believe it myself, but they made it impossible for me not to steal it. It was a challenge. What do I do now? I don't even smoke." I took it as a challenge, too.

While I was roving, an Indian couple in Seattle took me in, giving me food and shelter, treating me nice as if they had been my parents. The woman's name was Bonnie and we became close friends in no time. I managed to rip off the credit card of a very elegant-looking lady—the wife of an admiral. Ship ahoy! I at once took my friend to a fancy store and told her to take anything she wanted. I "bought" her about two hundred dollars' worth of clothes, courtesy of the navy. Another time I pointed out a similarly well-dressed woman to a store manager, saying, "I work for that lady over there. I'm supposed to take these packages to the car. She'll pay you." While the manager argued with the lady, I took off with the packages down the road and into the bushes.

Once I got a nice Indian turquoise ring, a bracelet, and a pin. I always admired the beautiful work of Indian artists, getting mad whenever I saw imitations made in Hong Kong or Taiwan. I learned to watch the storekeepers' eyes. As long as their eyes are not on you, you are safe. As long as they are not watching your hands. You can also tell by the manner in which they talk to you. If they concentrate too much on your hands, then they won't know what they are saying. It helps if you have a small baby with you, even a borrowed one. For some reason that relaxes their suspicions. I had no special technique except studying them, their gestures, their eyes, their lips, the signs that their bodies made.

I was caught only twice. The second time I happened to be in Dubuque, Iowa. That was after the occupation of Alcatraz, when the Indian civil rights movement started to get under way, with confrontations taking place between Indians and whites in many places. I had attached myself to a caravan of young militant skins traveling in a number of cars and vans. While the caravan stopped in Dubuque to eat and wash up, I went to a shopping mall, saw a sweater I liked, and quickly stuffed it under my Levi's jacket.

I got out of the store all right, and walked across the parking lot where the caravan was waiting. Before I could join it, two security guards nabbed me. One of them said, "I want that sweater." I told him, "But I don't have no sweater." He just opened my jacket and took the sweater from under my arm. They took me back to the office, going through my ID, putting down my name, all that kind of thing. They had a radio in the office going full blast and I could hear the announcer describing the citizens' concern over a huge caravan of renegade Indians heading their way. One of the guards suddenly looked up at me and asked, "Are you by any chance one of those people?"

"Yeah," I told him. "They're just half a mile behind me and they'll be here soon, looking for me."

He said, "You don't have to sign your name here. Just go. You can take that damn sweater too. Just get out of here!"

The incident made me realize that ripping off was not worth the risks I took. It also occurred to me there were better, more mature ways to fight for my rights.

Barb was less lucky. During the riots at Custer, South Dakota, she spent two days in the Rapid City jail. She was pulled in for third-degree burglary. It was the usual liberating of some food for which they were arrested, Barb and an Indian boy, but when she went before the judge and he told her that she was facing fifteen years, it made her sit up. She too started to reflect that if you had to go to jail it shouldn't be for a Saran-Wrapped chicken worth two bucks.

Most of the arrests occurred not for what we did, but for what we were and represented—for being skins. For instance once, near Martin, South Dakota, we had a flat tire and pulled off the road to fix it. It was late at night, dark, and very cold. While the boys were attending to the car, we girls built a good-sized fire to warm our backsides and make some coffee, coffee—pejuta sapa—being what keeps a roaming skin going. A fire truck went by. We did not pay any attention to it. A little while later the truck came back followed by two police cars. The police stared at us but kept on going, but pretty soon they made a U-turn and came back.

Across the road stood a farmhouse. The owner had called the police saying that Indians were about to burn his house down. All we were doing was fixing the tire and making coffee. The farmer had us arrested on a charge of attempted arson, trespassing, disturbing the peace, and destroying private property—the latter because in building our fire we had used one of his rotten fence posts. We spent two days in jail and then were found not guilty.

Little by little, those days in jail began adding up. We took such things in stride because they happened all the time, but subconsciously, I think, they had an effect upon us. During the years I am describing, in some Western states, the mere fact of being Indian and dressing in a certain way provoked the attention of the police. It resulted in having one's car stopped for no particular reason, in being pulled off the street on the flimsiest excuse, in being constantly shadowed and harassed. It works subtly on your mind until you start to think that if they keep on arresting you anyway you should at least give them a good reason for it.

I kept on moving, letting the stream carry me. It got to a point where I always looked forward to my next joint, my next bottle of gin. Even when the friends around me seemed to cool down I could not stop. Once I got hold of fifty white cross tablets—speed—and started taking them. The people I saw in the streets were doing it, why shouldn't I do it also? It gave me a bad case of the shakes and made me conclude that roving was not that much fun anymore. But I knew of no other way to exist.

Sexually our roaming bands, even after we had been politically sensitized and joined AIM, were free, very free and wild. If some boy saw you and liked you, then right away that was it. "If you don't come to bed with me, wincincala, I got some-body else who's willing to." The boys had that kind of attitude and it caused a lot of trouble for Barb and myself because we were not that free. If we got involved we always took it seriously. Possibly our grandparents' and mother's staunch Christianity and their acceptance of the missionaries' moral code had something to do with it. They certainly tried hard to implant it in us, and though we furiously rejected it, a little residue remained.

There is a curious contradiction in Sioux society. The men pay great lip service to the status women hold in the tribe. Their rhetoric on the subject is beautiful. They speak of Grandmother Earth and how they honor her. Our greatest culture hero—or, rather, heroine—is the White Buffalo Woman, sent to us by the Buffalo nation, who brought us the sacred pipe and taught us how to use it. According to the legend, two young hunters were the first humans to meet her. One of them desired her physically and tried to make love to her, for which he was immediately punished by lightning reducing him to a heap of bones and ashes.

We had warrior women in our history. Formerly, when a young girl had her first period, it was announced to the whole village by the herald, and her family gave her a big feast in honor of the event, giving away valuable presents and horses to celebrate her having become a woman. Just as men competed for war honors, so women had quilting and beading contests. The woman who made the most beau-tiful fully beaded cradleboard won honors equivalent to a warrior's coup. The men kept telling us, "See how we are honoring you . . ." Honoring us for what? For being good beaders, quilters, tanners, moccasin makers, and child-bearers? That is fine, but . . . In the governor's office at Pierre hangs a big poster put up by Indians. It reads:

WHEN THE WHITE MAN
DISCOVERED THIS COUNTRY
INDIANS WERE RUNNING IT—
NO TAXES OR TELEPHONES.
WOMEN DID ALL THE WORK—
THE WHITE MAN THOUGHT
HE COULD IMPROVE UPON
A SYSTEM LIKE THAT

If you talk to a young Sioux about it he might explain: "Our tradition comes from being warriors. We always had to have our bow arms free so that we could protect you. That was our job. Every moment a Pawnee, or Crow, or white soldier could appear to attack you. Even on the daily hunt a man might be killed, ripped up by a bear or gored by a buffalo. We had to keep our hands free for that. That is our tradition."

"So, go already," I tell them. "Be traditional. Get me a buffalo!"

They are still traditional enough to want no menstruating women around. But the big honoring feast at a girl's first period they dispense with. For that they are too modern. I did not know about menstruating until my first time. When it hap-pened I ran to my grandmother crying, telling her, "Something is wrong. I'm bleed-ing!" She told me not to cry, nothing was wrong. And that was all the explanation I got. They did not comfort me, or give horses away in my honor, or throw the red ball, or carry me from the menstruation hut to the tipi on a blanket in a new white buckskin outfit. The whole subject was distasteful to them. The feast is gone, only the distaste has remained.

It is not that a woman during her "moontime" is considered unclean, but she is looked upon as being "too powerful." According to our old traditions a woman during her period possesses a strange force which could render a healing ceremony ineffective. For this reason it is expected that we stay away from all rituals while menstruating. One old man once told me, "Woman on her moon is so strong that if she spits on a rattlesnake, that snake dies." To tell the truth I never felt particularly powerful while being "on my moon."

I was forcefully raped when I was fourteen or fifteen. A good-looking young man said, "Come over here, kid, let me buy you a soda"—and I fell for it. He was about twice my weight and a foot taller than I am. He just threw me on the ground and pinned me down. I do not want to remember the details. I kicked and scratched and bit but he came on like a steamroller. Ripped my clothes apart, ripped me apart. I was too embarrassed and ashamed to tell anyone what had happened to me. I think I worked off my rage by slashing a man's tires.

Rapes on the reservations are a big scandal. The victims are mostly full-blood girls, too shy and afraid to complain. A few years back the favorite sport of white state troopers and cops was to arrest young Indian girls on a drunk-and-disorderly, even if the girls were sober, take them to the drunk tanks in their jails, and there rape them. Sometimes they took the girls in their squad cars out into the prairie to "show you what a white man can do. I'm really doin' you a favor, kid." After they had done with them, they often kicked the girls out of their cars and drove off. Then the girl who had been raped had to walk five or ten miles home on top of everything else. Indian girls accusing white cops are seldom taken seriously in South Dakota. "You know how they are," the courts are told, "they're always asking for it." Thus there were few complaints for rapes or, as a matter of fact, for forced sterilizations. Luckily this is changing as our women are less reluctant to bring these things into the open.

I like men as friends, like to socialize with them, to know them. But going to bed with one is a commitment. You take responsibility for each other. But responsibility in a relationship was not what our young men wanted, some ninety percent of them. They just wanted to hop in the sack with us. Then they'd be friends. If you didn't cooperate then they were no longer interested in you as a person. With some of them, their whole courtship consists in pointing at you and then back at their tent, sleeping bag, or bedroll, saying, "Woman, come!" I won't come that easily. So I was a lot by myself and happy that way.

Once I played a joke on one of our great macho warriors, a good-looking guy, a lady's man. Women were always swarming over him, especially white groupies. One night, during a confrontation in California, I was lying in my sleeping bag when the great warrior (and he is a great warrior, I don't call him that facetiously) suddenly came up: "I had a little fight with my old lady. Can I share your sleeping bag?"

He did not wait for an answer but at once wedged himself in. This happened before Wounded Knee when I was in my eighth month. He put his hand upon my breast. I did not say anything. Then his hand wandered farther down, coming to a sudden stop atop that big balloon of a belly. "What in hell is this?" I smiled at him very sweetly. "Oh, I'm just about to have my baby. I think I feel my birth pangs coming on right now!" He got out of the sleeping bag even faster than he had crept in.

One Sioux girl whose lover had left her for a Crow woman was making up forty-niner songs about him. Forty-niners are songs which are half English and half

Indian, common to all tribes, often having to do with love and sometimes funny or biting. We were always singing them while we were on the move. So that girl made up this one:

> Honey, you left me for to go,
> Crow Fair and Indian Rodeo,
> Hope you get the diarrhea,
> Heya—heya—heya.

It became a great favorite with us, though I don't remember all of it. One song was all Indian except for the refrain: "Sorry, no pizza today." But to sum up: our men were magnificent and mean at the same time. You had to admire them. They had to fight their own men's lib battles. They were incredibly brave in protecting us, they would literally die for us, and they always stood up for our rights—*against outsiders!*

Sexual harassment causes a lot of fights between Indians and whites. Our boys really try to protect us against this. At Pierre, South Dakota's state capital, during a trial of AIM Indians, a lot of us came to lend our moral support, filling the motel, eight to ten people in a room. Barb was with a group occupying three rooms on the ground floor. On her way out to go to the car for some stuff, she passed three cowboy-type white boys leaning against a wall drinking beer and wine. Barb said she could smell the liquor on their breath from some ways off. They at once hemmed her in, making their usual remarks: "Look at the tits on that squaw. Watch her shaking her ass at us. I bet we could show that Injun squaw a good time," speculating aloud how it would be having her. My sister tried to ignore them, but in the end just turned around and ran back into the motel. The only one she could find there was Tom Poor Bear, an Oglala boy from Pine Ridge. Barb told him that some honkies had been harassing her outside. Tom at once went out with her and these cowboys again started with the same kind of shit, the same sort of sexual harassment. When they noticed Poor Bear they slowly began walking off. Tom called to them, "Hey, you guys come back and apologize."

The cowboy who had made the most offensive remarks turned around and fingered Poor Bear. He was grinning. "I don't apologize to her kind ever. She's nothing but a squaw."

Poor Bear told him, "You motherfucker, I'll show you who's nothing!" Then the fight started, all three of them jumping Tom, stomping him, three wasicuns against one skin. So again Barb scrambled back into the motel and in the lobby ran into Bobby Leader Charge, a Rosebud boy who was only fifteen years old at the time. Young as he was, Bobby just came out of that lobby like a thunderbolt, according to Barb, and joined the fight. By that time the cowboys had been reinforced by three more friends and again we were badly outnumbered. They were beating up on Poor Bear and Leader Charge, really hurting them, kicking them in the groin, going after their eyes. So once again Barbara was trying to round up more help. Luckily, at that moment Russel with the Means brothers and Coke Millard appeared at the motel. The whole sling of them rushed out. The honkies tried to get away, but were not fast enough. Coke Millard knocked one of them right over the top of a parked car. One cowboy got knocked out, just lying there. Another tried crawling away on his hands and knees. The others had run for it. This finished the incident as far as our men were concerned, and all went back to the motel.

But it was not finished. In no time the whole motel was lit up with searchlights as about half a dozen squad cars pulled up in front of it with their red lights flashing and sirens howling. Out of each car stepped two troopers with riot guns, helmets, and plastic shields, positioning themselves at both sides of each car. Already the loudspeaker was blaring: "This is the sheriff speaking. You Indians in there, you are wanted for assault and battery. We know you're in there. Come on out with your hands on your heads or we'll come in shooting!" Barb and the others peeked out from behind their window shades. Seeing the muzzles of all those riot guns and sawed-off shotguns pointing at them, they had little desire to come out. South Dakota police are notoriously triggerhappy when dealing with Indians, especially AIM people. One of the Means brothers went to the telephone and called up a white friend of ours who was in an upstairs room with one of the lawyers, helping with the trials. He told him to get his ass down to their room double quick, to bring the lawyer, and please, not to ask any foolish questions, just to hurry up.

It was two o'clock in the morning and very cold. Somehow it is always exceedingly hot or very, very cold in South Dakota. So, looking down from my room on the second floor I saw the two of them shivering, none too happy walking between the motel wall and the row of squad cars and troopers pointing their guns. Then I saw two pairs of hands reaching for them out of Room 108 and yanking them inside. I did not know at the time what it was all about. Barbara told me later that the two of them started negotiating by phone with the sheriff saying, "Our Indian friends and clients have been assaulted by a bunch of vicious, white, drunken, would-be rapists, but they are willing to withdraw these charges if your cowboys withdraw theirs."

While they were arguing back and forth on the phone, the others had a little problem with Coke, who had consumed a few beers and was singing his death song: "It's a good day to die! Let me out of here! I want to die a warrior's death. Let me count coup on them pigs! Hoka-hay!" They had to hold him back, literally sitting on him in order to keep him from going outside and getting himself killed. In the end both sides agreed to withdraw charges and call it quits to prevent a massacre. The squad cars drove off and all was quiet again, but it had been a near thing. There is always the danger for us that one little incident will set off a major confrontation.

Looking back upon my roving days, it is hard to say whether they were good or bad, or whether I accomplished or learned anything by being endlessly, restlessly on the move. If nothing else, my roaming gave me a larger outlook and made me more Indian, made me realize what being an Indian within a white world meant. My aimlessness ended when I encountered AIM.

Sioux and Elephants Never Forget

Now, in many ways the Sioux are prudes. They have a horror of nudity. They are in a way bashful. Boys and girls feel inhibited about showing affection for each other. Their fear of incest and the taboos connected with it are so severe that in traditional families a son-in-law will never speak to his mother-in-law, while a father-in-law will not behave in a familiar, easygoing way with a daughter-in-law. On the other hand the approach of a man to a woman is very simple and direct, and sex is taken for granted, as something natural or even sacred. Also medicine men are not supposed to be holier than other people, or sanctimonious like white Sioux and Elephants preachers. As old Lame Deer used to say, "They respect me not because I am such a good boy, but because I have the power." When it comes to women, medicine men are supposed to behave like everybody else.

I met Leonard at the Rosebud Fair and Rodeo. He took me for a ride in his old red convertible. Suddenly he had his arm around me and was kissing me. We were going to a party. I did not want to stay long. I did not want to be with him. I wanted to leave. I had a date with a young man from Oklahoma. But Leonard grabbed me by the arm and somehow maneuvered me out of the house down to the pasture, lifting me across the fence. Nobody was there. So in the end I went home with him. But I had not made up my mind about him. I was not ready to be tied down. So the next day I told his mother that I was going away, to another state. She said that Leonard had told her that I would be his wife for sure. I told her that I was not right for him. And I did not stay with him then. That came later.

At Sun Dance time Leonard approached me. He said he needed my help and my family's pickup truck to go into the hills for tipi poles. I went and borrowed a pickup from my brother-in-law. Leonard took me way up to the highest hill. It was pretty up there. I stood and looked around, admiring the beautiful view of the whole valley of the Little White River spread out before us. But there were neither tipi poles on that hill nor lodgepole pines. Leonard said, "Give your uncle a kiss." I kissed him. We stayed up on that hill for a considerable time. Again he asked me to be his wife, and once more I told him, "No, I won't."

After Wounded Knee, on the day the AIM leader Clyde Bellecourt was shot, we all got him to the hospital in the town of Winner where he was operated upon. Leonard was there and old Lame Deer, to pray and smoke the pipe for him. Then we drove in a caravan back to Rosebud and the Crow Dog place where Leonard held a big ceremony for Clyde's recovery. Everybody vowed to drink no more and to quit the wild life. After the ceremony he asked me to stay. I said, "No, I am going to leave." He cornered me and would not let me go. Again and again he said, "Be my wife." My ride had left in the meantime and so I ended up staying—for good.

Years ago Old Man Henry, Leonard's father, had somehow gotten hold of an enormous truck tire, as tall as a man. He had put this near the entrance gate and painted on it in big white letters: CROW DOG'S PARADISE. This paradise, Crow Dog's allotment land, is beautiful. The Little White River flows right through it. It is surrounded by pine-covered hills. In the sky overhead one can see eagles circling. Sometimes water birds, sacred to the peyote people, fly over it with their long necks outstretched. There are horses to ride. Everywhere on this land one is close to nature.

The paradise is not just a one-nuclear-family place, but rather a settlement for the whole clan, the whole tiyospaye. In 1973, when I moved in with Crow Dog, it consisted of two main buildings. The biggest one was the house in which Leonard's parents lived. Old Man Henry had built it himself out of whatever odds and ends he had been able to find—tree trunks, rocks, parts of an old railroad car, and tar paper. Some windows were car windows from wrecked vehicles. It was large with a big, old-fashioned iron stove, an old woodburning kitchen range, and an ancient, foot-powered sewing machine. Herbs, sacred things, and feather bustles hung down from the beams of the ceiling which was held up by two tree trunks. Right at the entrance stood the bucket with cool fresh spring water with the dipper for everyone to use. Coffee was always brewing on the range. On the outside Henry had painted the whole structure sky-blue with red trimmings. Nothing was at a right angle. Everything was bulging or sagging somewhere. There was no other house like Henry's. It stood for forty years and all Henry's children and most of his grandchildren were raised in it. It burned down under suspicious circumstances in 1976 while Leonard was in prison. Nothing is left of it now but the memory.

The other building is the one Leonard, I, and our children lived in. It was a flimsy thing, more in the nature of a bungalow than a house—a kitchen-living room and two tiny bedrooms. There was no cellar. The walls were thin and in winter it was hard to keep warm. It looks exactly like a few hundred other houses on the reservation built by the government under the OEO program. We call them "poverty houses." It is painted bright red and looks nice if you don't come too close.

There are always a few tipis around with people living in them, and somebody with no place to go who has made the outdoor cook shack his home. A white friend's camper was totaled a few years ago, and now a couple is using the shell for a home.

I now had a place and a man to stay with, but it was not always paradise in spite of the legend on the huge truck tire. I was in no way prepared for my role as instant wife, mother, and housekeeper. Leonard had three kids from his previous marriage—two girls, Ina and Bernadette, and one son, Richard. The girls were old enough to know that I was not their real mother, old enough to judge my performance. They had it in their power to accept or to reject me. I did not know how to cook. I did not even know how to make coffee. I did not know the difference between weak coffee and strong coffee, the kind that the Sioux like which will float a silver dollar.

Sioux always drop in on each other and stay over—a day or a week, as the spirit moves them. People eat at all times, whenever they are hungry, not when the clock says that it is eating time. So the women are continuously busy cooking and taking care of the guests. Indian women work usually without indoor plumbing, cook on old, wood-burning kitchen ranges, wash their laundry in tubs with the help of old-fashioned washboards. Instead of toilets we have outhouses. Water is fetched in buckets from the river.

Leonard is a medicine man as well as a civil rights leader. This means that we have ten times more guests than the usual Sioux household. The whole place is like a free hotel for anyone who cares to come through. The red OEO house in which I and Leonard live simply began to come apart from all the wear and tear. When I moved in, the place was a mess. Nobody tried to clean up or help out. They all came to eat, eat, eat, expecting a clean bed and maybe to have their shirts and socks washed. I spent a good many years feeding people and cleaning up after them. It is mostly men who stop by at the house, and only very few women, and you cannot tell men to do anything, especially Sioux men. I even sometimes moved my bed outside the house into the open to get some sleep, because the men stay up all night, talking politics, drinking coffee, and gossiping. Sioux men are the worst gossips in the world. I would wash dishes for the last time at midnight, go to bed, and in the morning all the dishes would be dirty again.

Most other medicine men do not go all out as Leonard does. They keep their homes tight, a little more to themselves. They do not fall into the trap of making their houses into dormitories and free hotels. Leonard pities people. Whenever we go to town we pick up somebody who is walking, and then usually we have him for dinner, and then breakfast. Some come and stay for days, weeks, or even months. Many Indians have no place to go, no one to feed them, so they come to Crow Dog's Paradise. If we see somebody who is out of gas, Leonard stops and siphons some off into his tank, and then we ourselves get stuck five miles from home. If Leonard notices someone having car trouble, he stops, takes out his tools, and fixes the car—an automobile medicine man on top of everything else. Money I am supposed to use for food or household things he gives away to anybody who asks. Years ago he got almost four thousand dollars in residuals for a TV commercial he did. That money was to buy a pickup truck. So, of course, there was a big giveaway feast. The friends and relatives—sixth cousins, seventh cousins, people very distantly related, strangers claiming kinship, one hundred and fifty of them—came. They came in rattletrap cars, in buggies, on horseback and muleback, on foot, in trucks. One came on a motorbike. Sides of beef were being barbecued. Women were engaged in an orgy of cooking. People went up to Crow Dog: "Kanji, cousin, I need a headstone for my little boy who died." "Uncle, I am crippled, I sit at home all day. I need a TV." "Nephew, my children need shoes." When the giveaway feast was over, Leonard had two dollars left to buy the pickup with.

Leonard's great-grandfather had seven wives to do the cooking and tanning and beading for giveaway feasts, and the buffalo meat was free, but those days are gone. Naturally, Leonard is much admired for his old-style Sioux generosity. At the Sun Dance of 1977 they put the war bonnet on him and made him a chief. They call him a wicasha waken—a holy man—but confidentially, it can be hell on a woman to be married to such a holy one.

Beside being tumbled headfirst into this kind of situation, still in my teens, with a brand-new baby and totally unprepared for the role I was to play, I still had another problem. I was a half-blood, not traditionally raised, trying to hold my own inside the full-blood Crow Dog clan, which does not take kindly to outsiders. At first, I was not well received. It was pretty bad. I could not speak Sioux and I could tell that all the many Crow Dogs and their relations from the famous old Orphan Band were constantly talking about me, watching me, watching whether I would measure up to their standards which go way back to the old buffalo days. I could tell from the way they were looking at me, and I could see the criticism in their eyes. The old man told me that, as far as he was concerned, Leonard was still married to his former wife, a woman, as he pointed out again and again, *who could talk Indian*. Once, when I went over to the old folks' house to borrow some eggs, Henry intercepted me and told me to leave, saying that I was not the right kind of wife for his son. Leonard heard about it and had a long argument with his father. After that there was no more talk of my leaving, but I was still treated as an intruder. I had to fight day by day to be accepted.

My own family was also against our marriage—for opposite reasons. Leonard was not the right kind of husband for me. I was going back to the blanket. Here my family had struggled so hard to be Christian, to make a proper red, white, and blue lady out of me, and I was turning myself back into a squaw. And Leonard was too old for me. I reminded them that grandpa had been twelve years older than grandma and that theirs had been a long and happy marriage. But that was really not the issue. The trouble was the cultural abyss between Leonard's family and mine. But the more our parents opposed our marriage, the closer became the bond between Leonard and myself.

I came to understand why the Crow Dogs made it hard for me to become one of them. Even among the traditional fullbloods out in the back country, the Crow Dogs are a tribe apart. They have built a wall around themselves against the outside world. For three generations they have lived as voluntary outcasts. To understand them, one must know the Crow Dog legend and the Crow Dog history.

Kangi-Shunka, the founder of the clan, had six names before he called himself Crow Dog. He was a famous and fearless warrior, a great hunter, a chief, a medicine man, a Ghost Dance leader, a head of the Indian police, and the first

Sioux—maybe the first Indian—to win a case before the Supreme Court. As Leonard describes him, "Old Kangi-Shunka, he was the lonely man of the prairie. He goes by the sun and moon, the stars and the winds. He harvests from the earth and the four-legged ones. He's a buffalo man, a weed man, a pejuta wichasha. He sees an herb and he hears the herb telling him, 'Take me for your medicine.' He has the kind of spirit and words out of which you create a nation."

For most people, what their ancestors did over a hundred years ago would be just ancient history, but for the Crow Dogs it is what happened only yesterday. What Kangi-Shunka did so long ago still colors the life-style and the actions of the Crow Dogs of today and of their relations, of the whole clan—the tiyospaye, which means "those who live together." Sioux and elephants never forget.

Some of the Crow Dogs trace their origin back to a certain Jumping Badger, a chief famous in the 1830s for having killed a dozen buffalo with a single arrow, for having counted fourteen coups in war, and for distinguishing himself in fifteen horse-stealing raids. It is certain that the first Crow Dog belonged to a small camp of about thirty tipis, calling themselves the Wazhazha or Orphan Band, which followed a chief called Mato-Iwa, Scattering Bear, or Brave Bear. Kangi-Shunka was born in 1834 and died in 1911. He was raised in the bow-and-arrow days when the prairie was covered with millions of buffalo and when many Sioux had still to meet their first white man. He died owning a Winchester .44 repeating rifle with not a single buffalo left to use it on. He lived long enough to ride in a car and make a telephone call. At one time he was a chief of the Orphan Band. He played his part in the proud history of our tribe.

As Old Man Henry tells it, Crow Dog got his name in this way: He was taking his people to Hante Paha Wakan, to Cedar Valley, to hunt. Before riding out he had a vision. He saw a white horse in the clouds giving him the horse power, and from then on his horse was Shunkaka-Luzahan, the swiftest horse in the band. And he heard the voice of Shunk-Manitu, the coyote, saying, "I am the one." Then his horse suddenly raised its two ears up and the wind got into the two eagle feathers Crow Dog was wearing, and the feathers were talking, the feathers were saying, "There is a wichasha, a man up ahead on that hill, between the two trees." Crow Dog and his companions saw the man clearly. The man raised his hands and suddenly was gone.

Crow Dog sent out two scouts, one to the north and one to the south. They came back saying that they had seen no one. Had this man on the hill been a wanagi, a spirit, trying to warn Crow Dog?

Crow Dog told his men to make camp near a river. He said, "Put the tipis close to the bank, so that the enemy cannot surround us." They did this. During the night Crow Dog could hear the coyote howl four times. Shunk-Manitu was telling him, "Something bad is going to happen to you." Crow Dog understood what the coyote was saying. Crow Dog got the men of his warrior society together, the Kit Foxes. They were singing their song:

> I am a fox.
> I am not afraid to die.
> If there is a dangerous
> deed to perform,
> That is mine to do.

They painted their faces black. They prepared themselves for a fight, for death.

At dawn the enemy attackedwhite settlers led by a white and many Crow scouts, with many Absaroka warriors helping them. With Crow Dog were many famous warriors. Numpa Kachpa was there, Two Strikes, who got his name when he shot down two white soldiers riding on the same horse with one bullet. Kills in Water was there, and Hollow Horn Bear's son, and Kills in Sight. Two Crows had wounded Kills in Sight and unhorsed him. Crow Dog came in on a run, killed the two Crows, and put Kills in Sight on his horse. He whipped the horse and it took off with Kills in Sight hanging on to it. The horse was fast and got Kills in Sight safely home.

Crow Dog was looking around, hoping to catch himself one of the riderless Crow horses, when he took two enemy arrows, one high on his chest right under the collarbone and the other in his side. He broke off the arrows with his hands. Hollow Horn Bear's son and two others of his men came to help him. They were wounded, and their horses all had at least one arrow stuck in them. Crow Dog told them, "I am hurt bad. I cannot live. No use bothering with me. Save yourselves."

They rode off. Crow Dog managed to get hold of a horse and got on it, but he weakened soon. He became so weak he fell off this pony. He was lying in the snow. He had hardly strength to sing his death song. Suddenly two coyotes came, trooping gently. They said, "We know you." They kept him warm during the night, one lying on one side and one on the other. They brought Crow Dog deer meat to make him strong, and they brought him a medicine. One of the coyotes said, "Put this on the arrow points." Crow Dog did what the coyote told him. The medicine made his flesh tender and caused it to open up so that he could take the arrowheads and what was left of the shafts out. They almost came out by themselves.

The medicine the coyotes gave him cured Crow Dog. The nourishment they brought him made him strong. The coyotes brought him home to his camp. A crow showed the way. Crow Dog said, "I was already walking on Ta-Chanku, on the Milky Way, on the road to the Spirit Land, but the coyotes led me back." And so he took on his seventh and last name, Kangi-Shunka, Crow Dog. Of course, it should have been Crow Coyote.

Years later, he was on his way to join Sitting Bull in Canada, and near the sacred Medicine Rocks he and his men were jumped by white soldiers. Crow Dog was hit by two bullets. His companions tied him to his horse and managed to get him home. This time a medicine man by the name of Sitting Hawk saved him. He told Crow Dog, "I will put my wound medicine into you. But I will not take the bullets out. One day you will die and go back to Mother Earth and the bullets will still be in you. Your human body will dissolve but the bullets will remain as evidence of what the wasicun have done to us."

This is the legend of Crow Dog, which Old Man Henry has told me many times. The first Crow Dog was a great warrior, though he never took part in a big battle, such as the Little Big Horn. He preferred to do his fighting as a member of a small war party made up of warriors from his own Orphan Band. He fought the wasicun and Pawnee and Crow warriors.

Crow Dog had been a close friend of Crazy Horse. Together with Touch the Clouds, White Thunder, Four Horns, and Crow Good Voice, he accompanied Crazy Horse when this Great Warrior surrendered himself at Fort Robinson in 1877. After Crazy Horse was treacherously murdered, it was Crow Dog's cool head and bravery which prevented a general massacre. As the enraged Sioux faced the soldiers who were only waiting for a pretext to start the killing, Crow Dog rode back and forth between them, pushing back the over-eager warriors and soldiers with the butt end of his Winchester.

Crow Dog was most famous for his having shot and killed Spotted Tail, the paramount chief of the Brule Sioux. They were cousins and when they were young, they had been friends. Later, their paths diverged. Spotted Tail said, "It's no use trying to resist the wasicun." He cooperated with the whites in most things. Crow Dog was like Sitting Bull; he stuck to the old ways. The so-called "friendlies" gathered around Spotted Tail, and the so-called "hostiles" around Crow Dog. This led to rivalry and rivalry led to trouble, big trouble that was slowly building up between the two men.

On August 5, 1881, Crow Dog was hauling wood in his buckboard with his wife beside him when he saw Spotted Tail coming out of the council house and getting on his horse. Crow Dog handed his wife the reins, took his gun, which was hanging beside him out of its scabbard, got down from his seat, and faced the chief. Spotted Tail saw him. He said, "This is the day we settle this thing which is between us like men." Spotted Tail went for his six-shooter. Crow Dog knelt down and fired, beating Spotted Tail to the draw. He hit the chief in the chest. Spotted Tail tumbled from his horse and died, the unfired six-gun in his hand. Turning Bear shot at Crow Dog's wife, but missed. Crow Dog drove back to his home with his wife. A man called Black Crow prepared a sweat lodge to purify Crow Dog. He loaded up the Winchester and shot it into the sacred rocks four times, saying, "Now Spotted Tail's spirit won't bother you." They then purified themselves with water.

A judge in Deadwood sentenced Crow Dog to be hanged. He asked leave to go home to prepare himself. The judge asked, "How do we know that you will come back?" Crow Dog said, "Because I'm telling you." The judge let him go. For a month Crow Dog prepared for his death. He made up a death song and gave all his things away. What little he had, his horses, wagon, chickens, he gave to the poor. His wife prepared a white buckskin outfit for him, plain, without beads or quillwork. He wanted to be hanged in this. When all was ready he hitched up his last horse to an old buggy and with his wife drove the one hundred and fifty miles to Deadwood for his own execution.

When he arrived at Deadwood his lawyer was waiting for him with a big smile: "Crow Dog, you are a free man. I went to the Supreme Court for you and the Court ruled that the U.S. government has no jurisdiction over the reservation and that there is no law for punishing an Indian for killing another Indian." Crow Dog said, "You're a damn heap good man. I have driven a hundred and fifty miles for nothing." Then he went home with his wife.

Black Crow told Crow Dog: "Cousin, the blood guilt will be upon you for four generations. From now on you will not smoke the pipe with other men. You will smoke a small pipe of your own, and you will smoke alone. You will not eat from a common dish; you will eat alone from your own bowl. You will drink from your own cup. You will not drink water from the dipper when it is handed around. You cannot eat from other people's dishes and they will not eat from yours. You will live apart from the tribe. Cousin, yours will be a lonely life."

Kangi-Shunka paid blood money. He gave the Spotted Tail family many horses and white-man dollars. That made peace between the families, but not between the Crow Dogs and the spirits. They suffered their ostracism with a certain arrogance. They were weighed down by Crow Dog's deed, but at the same time they were proud of it. Theirs was a proud sort of shame. The first Crow Dog was an outcast but also something of a hero. The Crow Dogs wrapped themselves in their pride as in a blanket. They turned guilt into glory. They began speaking of the royalness of their bloodline. The first Crow Dog had shown them the way. As a chief he had the right to wear a war bonnet, but he never did. Instead he found somewhere an old, discarded white man's cloth cap with a visor and to the top of it he fastened an eagle feather. And that he wore at all times—the lowest and the highest. He used to say: "This white man's cap that I am wearing means that I must live in the wasicun's world, under his government. The eagle feather means that I, Crow Dog, do not let the wasicun's world get the better of me, that I remain an Indian until the day I die." In some mysterious way that old cap became in the people's mind a thing more splendid than any war bonnet. And it was into this clan that I married.

The shock of having to deal at the same time with the myth and the reality, with trying to break through the Crow Dog buckskin curtain, and having to take care of the needs of so many people as well, was too much for me. I broke down. I got sick. I was down to ninety pounds. My body just collapsed. I could no longer stand up. If I tried, my legs would cramp up and hurt. My joints ached. I told Leonard, "I don't feel good. I can't sleep, and if I do I dream about people who have died, my dead friends and relations. Every time I close my eyes I see those who have been killed. I am sad, always. I think I am going to die too."

Leonard said he would do a doctoring meeting for me. He put up the peyote tipi for me. Another road man, Estes Stuart, came to help him. I ate the sacred medicine. I kept eating and eating. I was so weak I could not sit up. They made me lie down on a blanket. Leonard gave me some peyote tea to drink. It was old tea and very strong. I drank two whole cups of it. At midnight Estes prayed, and he talked while the water was going around. He said that since he was a peyote man he had X-ray vision, X-ray eyes which could see into my body, and he could not detect any sickness in me except one—love sickness. I felt so bad that tears came to my eyes. I thought, "Here I am, sick unto death, and they are making fun of me." I think I was a little paranoid. Estes had not been making fun at all. He explained later that what he meant was that mine was not a sickness of the body, but of the mind. That I felt that nobody loved me, not Leonard, not his family, not the people I cooked and washed for. I was sickening for want of love.

Suddenly people were all around me, talking to me, comforting me. Old Man Henry was patting my cheek, calling me "daughter." All those present were praying for me. All through the night I ate peyote. And Grandfather Peyote was calling me daughter.

When the sun rose, I rose too. I suddenly could sit up, even walk. I stepped outside the tipi and all around me I could see strange tropical birds flying, birds of metallic, fluorescent rainbow colors leaving trails of gold and silver. I went inside the house to lie down. I went to my bed, drew aside the blanket, and my legs turned to water. In my bed lay a strange woman, her hands crossed over her breast, her face stiff and white, her eyes unseeing. She was dead!

I got very scared. All of a sudden my whole body stopped. My heart quit pumping. My blood froze. I could not breathe.

Then I saw that the strange woman lying dead in my bed was me. Myself. And a great weight was lifted from me. I could breathe again. My heart was beating. I felt good. What was dying, what had died, was my former self, but I would go on living. Leonard came in and asked how was I doing. He put his arm around me and kissed me. He told me to lie down in the bed. As I did, the dead woman disappeared. The peyote power got hold of me. I started laughing. I kept on giggling and giggling. My ribs were sticking out, I had grown so skinny. I was all bones. But I kept on laughing for an hour. I would be all right.

Name _____

Date _____

Questions

From the writings of Gertrude Bonnin (Zitkala-Sa)

1. What are some of the primary cultural values of the tribal community in which Gertrude Bonnin spent the early years of her life?

_____

_____

_____

_____

_____

_____

_____

2. From the time she is taken by the missionaries to board the train ("the iron horse"), Bonnin begins to experience the alienation of the outsider. What does she seem to take from these experiences? In other words, how does she seem to internalize the messages she is given by the White world both on the train and in the boarding school? Answer this question, where possible, in terms of the psychology of oppression described in the introduction.

_____

_____

_____

_____

_____

_____

_____

3. Bonnin describes her years in the boarding school through a series of well-remembered incidents, few of which have to do with formal education. From those passages in her story, what can you surmise about the purposes that Indian boarding schools served both implicitly and explicitly?

_____

_____

_____

_____

_____

_____

4. Explore the stories of Bonnin's mother and brother. How did her relationships with and the experiences of each contribute to her ability to see the boarding school experience as she did?

_____

_____

_____

_____

_____

_____

_____

Name _____

Date _____

Questions

From the writing of Kay Redfield Jamison

1. In what way does Jamison's account of her life at college reflect how stigmatizing the mental illness of Bipolar Disorder can be?

_____

_____

_____

_____

_____

_____

_____

2. Compare Jamison's response to her condition to how you might respond to the same symptoms, knowing what you know now. Would you feel the same stigma she did? Do you think that our attitudes toward mental illness have changed since she began her struggle?

_____

_____

_____

_____

_____

_____

_____

3. In a different part of the book, Jamison describes her reluctance to take medication—("I simply did not want to believe that I needed to take medication" [p. 98]). This reluctance is endemic to many persons with chronic mental illness and has engendered a great deal of literature on "patient compliance with medical regimens." If you were to have a client such as Ms. Jamison, can you think of any ways in which she might be helped to take medication regularly and continuously?

_____

_____

_____

_____

_____

_____

_____

_____

_____

_____

_____

_____

Name _____

Date _____

Questions

Excerpt from Nancy Mairs

1. In this excerpt, Mairs refers to the social myths of the disabled woman. Can you think of any others besides those she has mentioned? If you were to be honest, to what extent do you personally subscribe to those myths? (For example, have you ever had an intimate relationship with a disabled person, or assumed that they were not as competent as you at tasks that had nothing to do with their disability?)

_____

_____

_____

_____

_____

_____

2. If you were a social worker whose job it was to work with persons with physical disabilities, how might it be different to work with someone who became disabled through a gradual process (as Mairs did), as opposed to someone who was suddenly disabled in an accident? How could you be most helpful?

_____

_____

_____

_____

_____

_____

_____

3. One of the recurring themes in the comments offered by Mairs and the other women concerns the need to be sexual. Clearly, this is an important issue for these women. How comfortable are you discussing sexuality in general? Would it be more difficult to discuss sexuality with a disabled person?

_____

_____

_____

_____

_____

_____

_____

_____

_____

_____

3 · THE PRACTICE OF SOCIAL WORK

WORKOUT 13 Assessing Clients' Strengths

If there is anything that one can get all social workers to agree on, it is the idea that client assessment is the heart of the helping process. For most traditionally trained social workers, this means that the client comes to the worker with a problem, and together the two work to ameliorate it. For the worker coming from an ecological perspective, this means altering the person, the environment, or both under the presumption that a better "fit" between the two is the desired end. For the behaviorally oriented worker, it means examining the "contingencies" in the environment that "maintain" the problem and changing them. Ironically, while nearly all models of practice speak of "client empowerment," it is clear that this empowerment is to be derived from focusing on a problem, overcoming that problem, and emerging victorious.

All of us at some time have experienced this: We had a problem, we overcame it, and we felt a clear sense of accomplishment as a result. Stated in more empowering terms, we had an aspiration, or a goal, and we used our strengths to meet it.

It is this latter sentence that states the essence of the strengths perspective in social work practice. Fundamental to this perspective is the assumption—the fact!—that everyone, regardless of their current situation or their personal characteristics, has hopes, dreams, and aspirations and may fulfill those only if they use their talents, abilities, and skills and the resources available to them.

Let us, for the moment, use you as an example to illustrate this. Suppose you are unemployed and need to find a job. After searching for some time, you find one. The hours are great, and the pay is not bad, although it is far away and you do not have a car. A problem-oriented social worker might see the problem as "how do we get you a car?" The strengths-oriented social worker, however, would reframe the question as follows:

"How do we help you meet your goal of employment at this job? What are the resources in the environment and your own personal strengths that will get you working at this place?" The distinction here is crucial: The former focuses on "the problem" (the lack of a car). Further, the implication that there is only one solution limits the possibilities. If we focus on the acquisition of a car, for example, we may fail to find out that (a) someone who works at or near this same place lives very close by and would be willing to take you to work for the price of half the gas; (b) you live on a bus route that gets you very close to the workplace; or (c) you are a highly skilled cyclist but need a better bike—a lot cheaper than a car!

To get at these other alternatives and in the process learn about the strengths in your repertoire, a worker might begin by asking you if you have ever been in a similar situation and how it was dealt with. If you have an older sibling who took you back and forth to work on your last job, great!

The author is particularly indebted to Charles A. Rapp, Associate Dean, University of Kansas School of Social Work, whose work in this area has moved so many to fundamentally change their ideas about social work practice.

A supportive sibling is a strength! So is your location in the community—on a bus route and/or living near someone who works nearby. There is also your expert cycling ability—a personal strength.

The same is true for clients: They have goals and aspirations that, when viewed through a problem lens, suggest narrow solutions. When viewed through an empowerment lens, however, previously uncharted possibilities emerge.

Sometimes clients have goals and aspirations that (a) you may not agree with or (b) you may believe are unrealistic. For example, a student I once worked with was using the strengths perspective with a client with severe and persistent mental illness. She was quite enthusiastic about the approach until she asked him what his goals and dreams were. Promptly, he replied, "I want to be a United States senator." "Delusions of grandeur," she thought. How am I supposed to apply a strengths perspective to a problem like this? She was stymied. She had expected him to say something more like, " I want to go to a Royals baseball game," which was at least in the realm of possibility. She brought her dilemma back to the class, which was encouraged to think using the strengths perspective. "Well, he should be applauded for having such high aspirations!" said one student. "All politicians are crazy," scoffed another, "so I don't see the problem." The student working with the client sank deeper into her chair. "Look," she said. "The guy is on a ton of meds. His hygiene is poor. He doesn't get out of his apartment much. Maybe I should just tell him to think of something else." Then a really quiet student spoke up:

> If his stated aspiration is truly what he wants, then he has handed you a gift. I think you should work with him on reaching this goal. In order to run for the Senate, he'll need to meet the public. To do that, he'll have to improve his hygiene. He'll need to read the newspaper and follow issues. He'll need to register to vote. All of these goals are important to the rest of his life! If he never becomes a senator, at least he'll have improved his hygiene, gone out and met a few people, and gotten more involved with the world. And who knows? Maybe he'll surprise all of us!

Now that's a strengths-oriented student! She accepted what the client had to say as a valid expression of what he wanted and told her classmate to start there. To do otherwise would have robbed the client of that which makes us human beings—our dreams.

Perhaps the most fully articulated strengths model in social work today is based on the work of Rapp (1997). Originally developed for use by case managers working with persons with serious mental illness, it has been successfully adapted for use with children (Benard, 1997) and the elderly (Fast & Chapin, 1997) as well as other populations. Rapp posits that the use of his strengths model is based upon the six cardinal principles discussed below. Read over these principles. Do you see how they could be (or were) applied in the examples given above?

Principle 1: The Focus Is on Individual Strengths Rather Than Pathology

This principle underscores the notion that people can grow and develop only when their strengths and opportunities are discovered and exploited. Focusing on diagnoses, pathology, and weaknesses may ground us in reality—we all have some of this, after all—but it does not help us progress. Thus, work with clients should be focused on what the client has accomplished thus far both in resources—personal and environmental—and in dreams and aspirations.

Principle 2: The Community Is Viewed as an Oasis of Resources

Individuals have strengths, but so too have environments. In this model, it is natural, or informal, resources that are preferred over more formal resources. For example, if you have children and need to work, you might find a baby-sitter or a nursery school. If you have limited funds, you might ask your mother or neighbor to care for your children, possibly in exchange for housework or yardwork on the weekends. Solutions such as these are preferable to federally funded child-care slots, for example, because this arrangement allows you to remain an integrated, involved member of the community. Furthermore, there is no stigma associated with this arrangement, as there is when formal income-maintenance resources are availed. Finally, the solution of bartering child care for house- or yardwork creates a relationship in which equity exists. Equity in relationships mitigates against resentment, embarrassment, or feelings of low self-esteem on the part of both principals in a relationship (Walster, Walster, & Berscheid, 1978).

Principle 3: Interventions Are Based on Self-Determination

The client has the right to determine the form, direction, and substance of the help desired. The professional works on behalf of the client and in partnership, and the client's goals, dreams, and aspirations become the center of the work.

Principle 4: The Worker-Client Relationship Is Primary and Essential

Much of social work practice stresses the importance of the client-worker relationship (Compton & Galaway, 1989; Perlman, 1979). Such relationships are sometimes difficult to establish: You are friendly but not a friend. You may be working on profoundly intimate goals with the client, but your boundaries are well established. Yet the relationship is terribly important. It is cooperative. There is trust. Sincere caring is there.

Principle 5: Aggressive Outreach Is the Preferred Mode of Intervention

This model of work with clients takes as a given that the best work with clients occurs in the less formalized settings of the client's environment. Asking the client to come to your office does several things: First, it deprives you of important sources of data. What is your client like in public? In what sorts of venues is that person comfortable? Second, the office is your turf, not the client's. It is a place where people who are either sick or poor or problem riddled come. Good things happen on neutral—or client—ground!

Principle 6: As Human Beings, We Are Capable of Learning, Growing, and Changing

This principle overlays the entire perspective. We all have a history of pain and problems as well as accomplishments, talents, dreams, and aspirations. To believe otherwise is to institutionalize low expectations; thus, this belief must be absolute.

Now that you know a little about one strengths model, the next step is to practice. That is what this workout is about.

WORKOUT 13 *Instructions*

Location

In class

Purpose

1. To provide you with opportunities to assess an individual, using elements of an empowerment perspective.
2. To give you the opportunity for some feedback about how you go about making those assessments.

Background

Assessment in general is more difficult than you might think. And a strengths-based assessment is, I submit, doubly difficult because of the orientation of our society to problems (to be solved), pathologies (to be treated), and faults (to be overcome). It is simply not part of our worldview to focus on strengths.

This workout requires you to practice assessment using the strengths perspective on one of your fellow classmates. Given that your classmates are not clients and given that the workout is to be done in the classroom, you will not be able to put all of the principles and ideas into action. This is, however, a beginning on which you can build your own assessment expertise.

Directions

1. Select a partner with whom you wish to conduct this exercise. If there are an odd number of students, one group may operate as a triad, with members taking turns as observers.
2. The Workspace includes a strengths assessment template that requires you to assess your "client" in six domains: living arrangements, financial/insurance, vocational/educational, health, leisure time activity, and social support. These domains, broadly conceived, constitute all the areas of our lives, so if you are conducting the assessment, begin by asking about one of these domains. For example, you might start with "Where do you live?" (the answer would fit most appropriately in the "Living Arrangements/Resources Available" cell). Next ask if that person likes where he or she lives, or if there is somewhere else she would like to be. That answer would fit in the "Interests and Aspirations" cell if the client would like to be elsewhere. The "needs" cell would contain the answer to the question "What kinds of things would you need to help you meet this goal?"

   The assessment is meant to be conversational. You need not discuss each of these domains in lockstep order. Nor should you worry too much about whether an expressed aspiration belongs more appropriately in one category or another (e.g., if someone were to say "I wish I had more friends up here at the university to do things with," that would fit in the center column of either the "Social Support" or the "Leisure Time Activity" category.

When you have completed this activity, make a list of the "goals" at the bottom of the page.

3. When you are undertaking the role of the client, you should take the opportunity to think about things in your life you would like to change and discuss them. If, for example, you wish your study habits were better, by all means state that to your "social worker." I recommend, however, that you monitor yourself and do not tell your classmate anything you would not want discussed after the exercise is over.

4. After one person has had ample time to conduct the assessment, the person in the role of the client should provide the worker with feedback, based on the feedback sheet, at the end of this exercise. Similarly, this process should take place when the roles are reversed, for the benefit of the other person to play the social worker.

This feedback sheet, on which you should take a moment to write comments, should be given to the person playing the social worker for future reference.

5. If your group has a third person, this person should also have the opportunity to conduct an assessment as a worker. The other group members can undertake the very valuable task of monitoring the assessment as it happens and sharing feedback with the worker at the end of the role-play.

WORKOUT 13 *Workspace*

Strengths Assessment

Resources Being Used and Involvements	Resources Available	Interests and Apirations	Needs
Living Arrangements			
Financial/Insurance			
Vocational/Educational			
Health			
Leisure Time Activity			
Social Support			
Personal Characteristics			

Feedback Sheet

Name _____

Date _____

For the benefit of _____ ("social worker")

1. Did the social worker use empowering language? Ask about your wishes? What you would like to see accomplished?

   _____

   _____

   _____

   _____

   _____

2. Did the social worker accept your goals, or try to direct you to less ambitious ones, or ones that were less desirable from your perspective?

   _____

   _____

   _____

   _____

   _____

3. Was the social worker facilitative? Did he or she encourage you to talk?

   _____

   _____

   _____

   _____

   _____

4. Did you both, despite your best efforts, lapse into a discussion of problems? (This is a very natural thing to do!)

_____

_____

_____

_____

5. To the extent that resources for meeting the goals were discussed, did the social worker suggest informal resources? (For example, if you told your worker you need a winter coat but you need money to buy it, did the worker suggest asking your relatives if any of them has a coat they don't use much, or to look through garage sales for a good, cheap coat?).

_____

_____

_____

_____

6. Was the social worker respectful and attentive? If you are of different cultural backgrounds, did the worker make an effort to understand how your culture might impinge upon your goals?

_____

_____

_____

_____

7. As a result of this workout, do you see yourself as having more strengths than you thought you had?

_____

_____

_____

_____

WORKOUT 14 Illuminating Research
Participant Observation

If you or your family have ever faced financial insecurity or even unrelenting poverty, if you have ever found yourself needing public assistance or food stamps, or if you have ever had to drop out of school because you simply could not afford it, then the debates over "welfare reform" and poverty policy in 1995 and 1996 were probably an epiphany for you. They certainly were for me. As a social worker with experience working with clients who find themselves in such circumstances, I listened to these debates with great interest and found myself wondering just who all these policymakers were talking about. Their assumptions about people on welfare simply did not square with most of my experience of people on welfare nor with that of my colleagues.

A similar experience for many occurred in 1991, as the nation sat glued to the television, watching Anita Hill give testimony to the Senate Judiciary Committee in the Clarence Thomas Supreme Court confirmation hearings. While women watched in amazement as Thomas was confirmed to the highest court in the land, the phrase "they just don't get it," used to describe the affluent White males who voted for confirmation, was repeated like a mantra. Meanwhile, many in the African American community agreed with Thomas, who described his confirmation experience as a "high-tech lynching."

Such experiences seem to confirm the validity of the emergence of standpoint theory, a sociological theory that assumes that all knowledge develops from the objective reality of people's lives (Hartsock, 1987; Swigonski, 1993). We are all grounded by our place in society, and our place in society is grounded by our gender, race, and/or class. Standpoint theory literally means that reality depends on "where you stand." And if you are non-White, nonmale, and poor, the "point" on which you stand is on the margins of society, where the view of reality is going to be very different from the view at the center.

Of course, the standpoint from which reality is viewed is ever shifting. Some White men are more marginal than others, due to class differences, for example, whereas affluent Black women may see reality differently when viewed through a racial lens than through a gender or class lens.

Believing in the validity of standpoint theory requires us to question "how we know what we know," to discontinue our almost exclusive reliance on externalized forms of knowledge, and to get "inside the skin" of those we seek to help as much as we possibly can. In doing so, we begin to lose the arrogance acquired in our lives of privilege, and we become better listeners to those who are actually experiencing the problem in question.

We become more empathic—a hallmark of a good social worker—in the process.

The purpose of this workout is to help you occupy the ground on which clients so often find themselves, if only for a short while.

I am indebted to Anthony Bibus, Chair of the BSW Program at Augsburg College, Minneapolis, Minnesota, for allowing me to use his ideas in this workout.

Location

In and outside class (small groups)

Purpose

1. To begin to expand your "standpoints" by constructing an experience you may not have encountered before.
2. To enable greater development of empathy for those we serve in a professional capacity.

Background

One of the most profoundly knowledge-expanding activities a person can undertake is the immersion in an experience that person would not normally be privy to in the course of everyday life. When this is done in a rigorous, organized way, it is called *participant observation*. Some of our most influential studies in sociology have used this method of knowledge building very effectively. For example, Carol Stack (1974) explored the experience of life in an extremely impoverished midwestern African American community by moving into a house there for two years. Her book, *All Our Kin,* paints a profoundly rich portrait of the lives of her neighbors. Similarly, Sue Estroff (1981) lived the life of a client with chronic mental illness living in Madison, Wisconsin and effectively exposed the difficulties of that life and the problems associated with service delivery vacuums and the side effects of psychotropic drugs.

Your task in this workout is to engage in a very limited exercise in participant observation. As with all such studies, the greater the immersion in the experience, the more meaningful, both to you and to those to whom you disseminate your findings (in this case, your classmates and instructor).

Directions

1. In all the dialogues and debates on "welfare reform," one idea that seems to surface more than almost any other is the application of pressure on recipients to find a job as quickly as possible. That job should preferably lead to self-sufficiency, although many policymakers argue that any job is preferable to public assistance. One aspect of finding a job, of course, is the job interview and the preparation necessary for that interview, which includes dressing appropriately. This workout requires you to conduct a participant observation related to using limited resources to prepare for a job interview. Begin by breaking into groups of two or three.
2. Go as a group to one or more of the thrift stores (i.e., Goodwill Industries, Salvation Army, St. Vincent de Paul, etc.) in your community and select an ensemble (i.e., suit, pantsuit, or dress along with shoes) that you think would be appropriate for a job interview for one member of your group. All members of the group should agree on the appropriateness of this outfit.

3. While there, observe as much as you can without being obtrusive. Notice who else is there—their age, sex, and so forth.

4. Monitor your own feelings. If you have never shopped in such a store, mentally note your own feelings about the experience, and jot them down in the Workout 14 Workspace.

5. Purchase the items you have selected. The cost, divided between members of the group, should be nominal. Save the price tags and note the total in the Workspace.

6. At a time designated by your instructor, the person for whom the clothing was purchased should "model" the outfit for the rest of the class. At that time, the group should discuss how they felt about their experience. In particular, how did the "model" feel about the experience of wearing the clothes on campus?

For this assignment to be fully effective, the following rules must be observed:

- Do not wear expensive clothing or jewelry on this assignment.
- If any salespersons approach, tell them you are looking for something suitable for a job interview. **DO NOT** say "I am here as a class assignment" or otherwise imply that you somehow do not really belong. Such behavior would be disrespectful to the other customers, who do not have the option of going elsewhere.
- If you are the person designated to wear those clothes, wear them with dignity. Do not tell those on the bus on the way to school "I had to do this for a class," for example. Again, our clients have no such option.

In fact, a good rule to guide your behavior is to observe yourself and ask yourself if what you are doing is something that a client would be equally able to do.

Alternative Assignment

If you already have firsthand knowledge of the experience noted above, you may wish to undertake a different experience. Here are some suggestions to consider:

- If there is a clubhouse or day treatment program for persons with serious mental illness in the community, you may wish to observe there. If such a program is housed in an agency, attaining permission is going to be very important.
- Many communities have open meetings of Alcoholics Anonymous that persons who are not chemically dependent can attend. Check with a drug treatment agency in your community about this.
- Some public child welfare agencies sponsor meetings for prospective adoptive parents. Attend a meeting. Listen to the questions asked as well as to what people reveal about themselves.

WORKOUT 14 *Workspace*

Name _____

Date _____

1. The place you went to purchase your job interview clothing was

   _____

2. About how difficult was it to find something for the person in your group to wear?

   ____ Very difficult   ____ Somewhat difficult   ____ Somewhat easy   ____ Very easy

3. What was the itemized cost of this outfit?

   Item 1: _____   Cost: _____

   Item 2: _____   Cost: _____

   Item 3: _____   Cost: _____

                                             Total: _____

4. Describe your feelings about this experience. How did you feel while you were engaged in this task? What were your thoughts and reflections afterward?

   _____

   _____

   _____

   _____

   _____

   _____

   _____

   _____

   _____

   _____

5. In what way does this experience increase your understanding of those who have limited choices and are required, by financial exigencies, to do exactly what you did?

_____

_____

_____

_____

_____

_____

_____

_____

_____

_____

_____

_____

_____

_____

_____

_____

_____

_____

_____

_____

WORKOUT 15 Acquiring Goods and Services for Clients
Resource Acquisition

Once a social worker has made a careful, thorough assessment of the client's needs and strengths, a plan is developed that articulates how these needs will be met. An experienced social worker will also be able to anticipate barriers, or obstacles, to meeting these needs and develop strategies for overcoming those barriers. For example, suppose that you are working with a female client and her two children. She has resolved to leave her abusive partner but has nowhere to go. As her social worker, you have found a shelter that currently has room for her and her children, but you are mindful of the fact that, after 30 days, she will need to move somewhere else because the shelter has a 30-day occupancy limit. Knowing this allows both you and the client time to explore other options and marshal other resources so that this transition may be made more smoothly.

Regardless of one's practice orientation, good practice usually dictates that, when seeking to assist clients in acquiring resources, the social worker begins with the most *informal* sources of help before proceeding to the more *formal*. This continuum of resources may be conceptualized as follows:

- *Personal:* The client's own strengths as well as the talents, abilities, and material assistance that family, friends, or work colleagues may be able to provide
- *Community:* Neighbors, informal self-help groups, grassroots advocacy organizations, or other locally organized entities, such as informal parent groups
- *Institutional:* Churches, schools, and other quasi-formal organizations
- *Formal:* Public social services, local agencies, and other organizations that exist to meet specific needs

There are many reasons why social workers use this general model of resource acquisition. First, to the extent that a source of help tends toward the formal end of the continuum, it is more rigid and bureaucratized. For example, many quasi-formal and formal organizations have strict limits on the number of times a person may access their resources, and the person may be required to offer proof of need (rent receipts, utility bills or receipts, medical records, etc.). While such documentation requirements are understandable from these organizations' point of view, the resultant lack of privacy may be so embarrassing and stigmatizing that the client avoids this source of help altogether.

Other barriers to resource acquisition may also exist. Suppose our hypothetical client, housed in the shelter with her children, had a job ? That job may now be more important than ever for her financial stability, but the shelter, unlike her house, is not on a bus route and she has no transportation. Alternatively, what if she finds an apartment that is on a bus route and is of adequate size, but the landlord demands a month's rent and a deposit against damage equaling an additional month's rent?

You are asked to keep these ideas in mind as you complete the following workout. Not only will it afford you an experience in resource acquisition, but it should also increase your understanding of the difficulties that clients encounter as a result of their dependence on more formal systems of support.

WORKOUT 15 *Instructions*

This exercise was originally developed by Harold Richman, a renowned social work scholar at the University of Chicago, and adapted for use here.

Location

Outside class

Purpose

1. To introduce you to the real experiences of people who find themselves in a position of dependency.
2. To help you learn more about the resources available for certain types of clients in your community, the gaps in the resources needed by clients, and the barriers to attaining those resources.

Background

Linking clients to needed resources is one of the most important aspects of social work. Because resources often come from informal sources, this exercise assumes that family and friends are unavailable to help with this problem and that the client must rely on more formal sources (i.e., clubs, agencies, and organizations).

The best social workers, by virtue of their experience, have a keen understanding of where and how needed resources are most likely to be attained. They are also dogged and persistent. In other words, they follow a resource lead to its conclusion.

Directions

1. Below are four vignettes, each describing a person or persons with a different problem. Choose *one* of these vignettes.
   a. Christine, a 15-year-old sophomore in high school, seeks you out because a home-pregnancy test reveals that she is pregnant. She has had sex twice with a boyfriend who is aware of her plight. Christine was raised in a very religious home and in the past has sought her pastor out for problems. However, she has never had a problem like

---

this and is not willing to do so now. She is deeply fearful of the reaction her parents would have to this news. She does not know what she wants to do, but she does know that she wants as much information as possible about the options available to her and wants to make this decision for herself.

Help Christine make an informed decision by providing her as much information as you can find about all the options available to her. How would you help her access the resources she needs for the decision she ultimately makes (for the purposes of this assignment, assume a decision on her part).

b. Harry, a 57-year-old male, recently received the results of some medical tests done during a recent hospitalization. He has Alzheimer's disease, and although it is currently manageable, Harry will inevitably get worse. The doctor has predicted that within a year, Harry will need monitoring on a fairly constant basis and will not be left alone for more than a few hours at a time.

At the present time, Harry is cared for by his wife, Louise, who works part-time for $5 an hour (less than 20 hours per week). Harry has worked in a scrap yard for the past 7 years at $7 an hour full-time. However, given the progression of his illness and the mental acuity required to operate the heavy machinery in the yard, his boss has made a decision to relieve him of his job. Harry and Louise have one grown child, who lives in another state.

What can be done for Harry and Louise that will allow both to live their lives as normally as possible? In other words, what service options are available for Harry and Louise now, and what will his options be in the future as his health deteriorates?

c. Your cousin, Mickey, 28 years old, dropped out of high school 3 months short of his high school graduation because his thoughts were jumbled up and he heard "voices" when no one was there. His parents took him to a psychiatrist, who diagnosed him as having mild paranoid schizophrenia. Since that time, he has held many different jobs, most of which lasted only a few months. Failure to show up for work would inevitably lead to being fired. For the past 6 months, he has not been able to find any work, and his unemployment benefits have been exhausted. His landlord says he will let him stay for a while longer.

In the 10 years since the onset of his illness, Mickey was in the state hospital, but recently the closest one was closed. Besides, hospital personnel say he is not sick enough to be rehospitalized. The problem, they say, is lack of medication compliance: Mickey refuses to take prescribed medicine because he says it "dopes him up."

What can be done for Mickey?

d. Terry, a 12-year-old boy, lives in the public housing project with his mother. She receives monthly payments from Transitional Assistance to Needy Families (TANF), and food stamps. Recently, Terry's mother began a welfare-to-work program as a condition of continuing to receive TANF. Where she was once home when Terry got home from school, she is no longer able to be.

Terry has been an average student since starting school, but lately his grades have dropped precipitously. He has had a number of unexcused absences, and the teachers have also noted a dramatic change in his attitude and demeanor. His mother would like to understand what is going on and to get help for Terry if he needs it, but she is too busy now to really help.

How can Terry and his mother be helped?

2. Provide a very brief explanation of the social problem reflected in the vignette. What are the generally experienced needs of persons who suffer from this problem? What are the specific needs of the individual in this vignette? Is this problem created by environmental barriers, problems of character or personality of the individual, or both?

3. After you have determined the goods and/or services that this person might need, go about looking for ways to meet those needs.

[Note: Because the purpose of this workout is for YOU to gain experience, your instructor will not be providing you with much guidance. However, you may wish to start with the yellow pages of the phone book, a social worker you know in the community, or a public social service office.]

Keep a **dated** log of your efforts in the Action Log in the Workout 15 Workspace. What was the source of your information? What did you read? With whom did you speak? (name both the agencies/organizations with whom you spoke and the individual at the agency). How did they respond to your queries? Did they provide you with other references?

4. In the Workspace, list the options available for the person in the vignette. What is/are the systems (or lack thereof) that exist to help people in this situation? What choices would you make if this were happening to you or to others in your family? Why?

5. Are there resource systems that exist but are not accessible to your client? For example, are there long waiting lists for any of the services? Is the application process for the service complicated or cumbersome? Is there a sliding scale fee for the service that your client might still not be able to afford? Enter your ideas in the Workspace.

6. Finally, you may wish to discuss in class the outcome of this assignment. Is it easier or more difficult to meet the needs of people with serious problems, or is it about how you thought it would be?

Name _____

Date _____

The person whose vignette I have chosen to address is _____ (name).

1. Briefly, explain the **social problem** reflected in the vignette you have chosen.

   _____

   _____

   _____

   _____

   _____

2. In the spaces below, describe the **generally experienced needs** of people who find themselves in the same boat as the person in the vignette.

   _____

   _____

   _____

   _____

   _____

3. Describe the **specific needs of the individual** in the vignette.

   _____

   _____

   _____

   _____

   _____

4. What are the **community, organizational, or societal barriers** to solving this problem, if any?

_____

_____

_____

_____

_____

_____

_____

5. What are the barriers, if any, imposed by the individual or his/her family?

_____

_____

_____

_____

_____

_____

_____

6. What are some of the strengths that people can use to overcome those barriers?

_____

_____

_____

_____

_____

_____

_____

7. Complete the Action Log as you seek ways to meet the person's needs.

Action Log

No.	Date	Agency Called	How/Where Did You Find Out About This Resource?	Person You Spoke With	Response/Leads (other places they suggested you call)
1					
2					
3					
4					
5					
6					
7					

Action Log

No.	Date	Agency Called	How/Where Did You Find Out About This Resource?	Person You Spoke With	Response/Leads (other places they suggested you call)
8					
9					
10					
11					
12					
13					
14					

8. List the services/options available for the person(s) in your vignette. Then, if applicable, provide a list of services that would be very useful to the person but do not exist.

Services/ Options Available

Services Needed But Nonexistent

_____   _____

_____   _____

_____   _____

_____   _____

_____   _____

_____   _____

9. Given what you now know about what is available for persons in this situation, what choices would you make if this were happening to you? Why?

_____

_____

_____

_____

_____

_____

_____

_____

_____

_____

_____

_____

_____

10. Describe any access problems your client would be likely to experience with the services available to him/her. Access problems include waiting lists, geographically long distances to acquire the service, out-of-pocket expenses associated with obtaining the service, cumbersome application processes, regulatory restrictions, and the like.

_____

_____

_____

_____

_____

_____

_____

_____

_____

_____

_____

_____

_____

4 A VISION
   FOR THE FUTURE

WORKOUT 16 Caring for the Elderly in the 21st Century

As I write this workout, the news is full of the latest battle being waged in the halls of Congress: Should premiums and copayments for Medicare services be raised on America's highest-income citizens? Should any senior citizen have to pay $5 per home health visit? Should seniors whose income exceeds $50,000 for a single person, and $75,000 for a couple be required to pay an additional $13 per month toward their medical services? Strong disagreement exists between those who believe in health care for the aging as an entitlement and those who believe that senior citizens who are financially able should make a fair contribution to defraying our national debt.

Although these debates are likely to have an impact on all of us, we pay less attention to them than we do to the more personal issues of aging on our own home front. Perhaps you have one or more grandparents, currently living in their own home, who would require institutional care were it not for careful monitoring of their needs by your own parents. Or perhaps one or more of your grandparents died but not before requiring the near-constant ministrations of their children (among them your mother or father), which took a significant toll on your family life.

In either case, witnessing the aging process (a personal experience) and our national response to that process (a political experience) will have enormous repercussions on your life later on. How will you prepare for old age? Even more significant, what are you doing right now to prepare for old age? Are you prepared to meet the challenge of living on a retirement income? Potential dependence on others? Do you believe that Social Security will not be in existence when you reach retirement age? (Surveys reveal that many in "Generation X" hold this view.)

The primary purpose of this workout is to get you to think about the unthinkable: What will the world be like when I retire, and how should I prepare for it? Another purpose is to stimulate your thinking about some of the major issues on the plates of both gerontologists and those living those issues: persons who are elderly now.

WORKOUT 16 *Instructions*

Location

In and outside class

Purpose

1. To stimulate your thinking about current policy decisions that may impact your future as a senior citizen.
2. To provide you, as a beginning scholar in this field, a clearer sense of the concerns, feelings, and problems shared by the elderly in your community.

Background

Most of us find it difficult to discuss aging, particularly with someone who is already elderly. The gallows humor runs rampant, as do the references to false teeth (which many do not have), memory loss (which many do not have), and decreased sensory input (such as failing eyesight, which many do not have). Clearly, serious talk about aging, particularly with those close to us, remains taboo.

But have you ever wondered about the aging process? Wondered at what point your own grandparents realized that they needed to save some money for retirement, if ever? Or where they thought they would be at this point in their lives when they were your age? Have you ever asked them for any advice about what you should be doing now to prepare for the future? Is there anything they did (or did not do) in terms of long-range planning that they now regret?

Asking these questions not only helps you think about how you can be better prepared for the future but gives you some realistic idea of the problems and issues you might be dealing with as a social worker. For example, if in a conversation with your grandmother it was revealed to you that she is fearful of ultimately requiring placement in a nursing home (actually, only 5% of the elderly reside in nursing homes at any given time), you might then begin to think not only about services that can prevent such placement but about service gaps that could address such a problem. This is how issues begin to be addressed at both the personal and political levels—with a real experience that galvanizes one to action.

You may not be galvanized to act on what you learn from this workout right away, but I am hopeful that you will not forget it and use it to act on your own behalf, at the very least, or on behalf of others.

Directions

Using the Workout 16 Workspace designated for note taking, conduct an interview with a person who is at least age 70. Such a person is, in all likelihood, now living with the consequences of his/her own actions taken when younger. This person can be a grandparent, other family friend or relative, or someone you do not know well who is willing to share personal experiences with you.

Although this is not a formal interview, you should include these questions in the conversation (in no particular order):

1. How old are you presently?
2. Where, and with whom, do you currently live?
3. Are you satisfied with your current living arrangement? If not, where would you prefer to live? What prevents you from living where you prefer?
4. I am _____ (years old). Do you have any advice for me regarding what I should do to live a good older age?
5. Is there anything you could have done to better prepare yourself for older age, either economically or socially? Do you wish you had lived a healthier lifestyle, or is that relatively unimportant?
6. Do you believe that Social Security will be solvent when I am in my 60s? Do you believe there is a problem with Social Security?
7. What are some of the things (hobbies, avocations) that you like to do?
8. Does spirituality, or religion, play a role in your life, and is it greater or less than when you were younger?
9. (If you are discussing these ideas with a woman): Did you defer, as many women did, to your husband regarding financial matters, and if so, how as this impacted you now?
10. Do you watch the debates in Congress about matters affecting the elderly, and what is your opinion about those issues?

WORKOUT 16 *Workspace*

Notes From Interview

Once you have finished the interview, answer the following:

a. What did you learn about the aging process that had not occurred to you before?

_____

_____

_____

_____

_____

b. How is this new knowledge going to change your behavior?

_____

_____

_____

_____

_____

c. What would you say is the single most important action you/we can take to ensure, to the greatest extent possible, that you will have a "good aging"?

_____

_____

_____

_____

_____

_____

WORKOUT 17 Envisioning the Future of Social Work

One of the most common and interesting discussions I hear at social work conferences around the country has to do with the future—yours and mine. There is no doubt that social work is changing. With the passage of laws that radically alter the welfare system in every state, the advent of managed care systems to help contain the costs of health and mental health care, and (as I write this) the specter of the removal of universality from the Social Security system, the repercussions on the profession most often charged with negotiating these systems are inevitable.

In addition to economic and political changes, the racial and ethnic background of our country is changing too. Over the past several decades, we have undergone a radical shift from a predominantly Caucasian country to a truly multicultural one. In fact, demographers tell us that if current trends continue, the Hispanic population will soon become the largest ethnic population subgroup in the country.

Futurists are persons who forecast social, structural, and economic changes in our country and the world. Among the best known are Alvin and Heidi Toffler, who have written extensively about how the technology revolution will change our lives, and John Naisbett and Patricia Aburdene, who forecast the continuation of several developments begun in the past decade, including the privatization of the welfare state (1990). Recently, Reisch and Gambrill (1997) published a volume of essays by social work scholars on the future of the profession as well as a variety of social policies.

Haynes and Holmes (1994) also touch on some of the changes likely to occupy the attention of the profession well into the future: How will chronic care services for the elderly be delivered to the nation's burgeoning elderly population, and how will these services be paid for? Will women still have the right to control their own fertility? As privatization of social services becomes more prevalent and marketplace ideologies supplant the ideology of the welfare state, how will people who require or would benefit from services fare? What will be the impact of the cybernetic revolution (high tech) upon social work ("high touch")? (The implications for confidentiality, as well as the loss of human contact, are significant.)

As you approach your professional future, it is important to contemplate the changes likely to occur and the impact on the work you will be doing. Will the changes you foresee make a difference now in the way you prepare for your professional life? If so, now is the time to begin making these preparations.

Location

In class

Purpose

1. To help you think about the preparation necessary for a career in the social work profession of the future.
2. To give you an opportunity to project yourself where you want to be in the future and to help you set some goals for getting there.

Background

The fact that you are now working on the last workout in this book suggests that you have spent an entire semester learning about the profession of social work and social welfare. In this process, you have undoubtedly arrived at some conclusions about your potential place within this profession and how you relate to the institution of social welfare.

Now is the time to go a step further: What kind of professional social work do you see yourself doing in the next 5 years? The next decade? The next 20 years? And how are the changes that you foresee occurring in the environment likely to affect that work? If you do not contemplate a career in social work, where do you see the institutions that make up the social welfare system changing in those same time intervals? Will the social safety net, which has tightened so much over the past decade, reverse itself and gain strength? Or will the present course continue? How will changes in the care of our elderly affect our society? What will our policies toward immigration be like in the future? What will be the impact of the advent of new, more effective drugs to combat illnesses such as AIDS and serious mental illnesses such as schizophrenia?

The best thing about this workout is that you will not be graded on your accuracy. It is your imagination muscle that gets the best exercise here!

Directions

In the space below, write an essay about your future in social work (if you are not contemplating a career in social work, your instructor can help you adapt these questions so that they are more relevant to you). You may structure this essay any way you like, but you should include in it the following:

- What population would you like to be working with upon graduation? In what type of setting? Do you see your interests changing (with respect to either population or setting) within the next 5 years? The next decade?
- Given what you have read in the newspapers, discussed in school, and experienced in your own life, what kinds of structural changes do you think are likely to take place within society that will impact your work? For example, in the area in which you live, are more young people

moving away than are moving in? Or do you live in an area of rapidly increasing population growth? What are the implications of those population shifts? Do you live in an area with a large manufacturing base or a service economy? Is this changing? How? How will this impact the citizens, and subsequently your work?

- Does the work that you aspire to do anticipate these changes? For example, if you are working in an area with a lot of out-migration of the youth population, with children thus unavailable to take care of their aging parents, are you as a result anticipating a career in gerontological social work? Or, if your city is experiencing a large influx of new residents, an increase in the need for other social services is indeed possible. Are you thus preparing yourself to work in those fields?

- In general, do you think the need for social workers will increase, decrease, or remain the same over the next two decades? Explain.

WORKOUT 17 *Workspace*

Name _____

Date _____

I Am the Futurist: An Essay

_____

_____

_____

_____

_____

_____

_____

_____

_____

_____

_____

_____

_____

_____

_____

_____

_____

_____

_____

BIBLIOGRAPHY

Abbott, A. (1988). *Professional choices: Values at work.* Silver Spring, MD: National Association of Social Workers.

Addams, J. (1911). *Newer ideals of peace.* New York: Macmillan.

Addams, J. (1922). *Peace and bread in time of war.* New York: Macmillan.

Bartlett, H. (1958). The working definition of social work practice. *Social Work, 3*(2), 3-9.

Benard, B. (1997). Fostering resiliency in children and youth: Promoting protecting factors in the school. In D. Saleebey (Ed.), *The strengths perspective in social work practice* (2nd ed., pp. 167-182). New York: Longman.

Bulhan, H. A. (1985). *Franz Fanon and the psychology of oppression.* New York: Plenum.

Compton, B., & Galaway, B. (1989). *Social work processes* (4th ed.). Belmont, CA: Wadsworth.

Estroff, S. (1981). *Making it crazy: An ethnography of psychiatric clients in an American community.* Berkeley: University of California Press.

Fanon, F. (1968). *The wretched of the earth.* New York: Grove.

Fast, B., & Chapin, R. (1997). The strengths model with older adults: Critical practice components. In D. Saleebey (Ed.), *The strengths perspective in social work practice* (2nd ed., pp. 115-131). New York: Longman.

Hartsock, N. (1987). The feminist standpoint: Developing the ground for a specifically feminist historical materialism. In S. Harding (Ed.), *Feminism and methodology* (pp. 157-180). Bloomington: Indiana University Press.

Haynes, K., & Holmes, K. (1994). *Invitation to social work.* New York: Longman.

Hegel, G. W. F. (1966). *The phenomenology of mind.* London: Allen & Unwin. (Original work published 1807)

Hoffman, K., & Sallee, A. (1994). *Social work practice: Bridges to change.* Boston: Allyn & Bacon.

Horner, W. C., & Whitbeck, L. B. (1991). Personal vs. professional values in social work: A methodological note. *Journal of Social Service Research, 14,* 21-43.

Hoshino, G., & McDonald, T. (1975). Agencies in the computer age. *Social Work, 20,* 10-14.

Karls, L. M. (1992). Should social workers be licensed? Yes. In E. F. Gambrill & R. Pruger (Eds.), *Controversial issues in social work* (pp. 52-56, 64-65). Needham Heights, MA: Allyn & Bacon.

Lowell, J. S. (1997). The economic and moral effects of public outdoor relief. In J. Axinn & H. Levin (Eds.), *Social welfare: A response to human need* (pp. 111-113). White Plains, NY: Longman. (Original work by Lowell published 1890)

Mathis, T. P. (1992). Should social workers be licensed? No. In E. F. Gambrill & R. Pruger (Eds.), *Controversial issues in social work* (pp. 56-64). Needham Heights, MA: Allyn & Bacon.

Morales, A., & Sheafor, B. (1995). *Social work: A profession of many faces.* Needham Heights, MA: Allyn & Bacon.

Naisbett, J., & Aburdene, P. (1990). *Megatrends 2000: Ten new directions for the 1990s.* New York: William Morrow.

Perlman, H. (1979). *Relationship: The heart of helping people.* Chicago: University of Chicago Press.

Popple, P., & Leighninger, L. (1990). *Social work, social welfare, and American society* (3rd ed.). Boston: Allyn & Bacon.

Rapp, C. (1997). *The strengths model: Case management with people suffering from severe and persistent mental illness.* New York: Oxford University Press.

Reamer, F. (1993). *The philosophical foundations of social work.* New York: Columbia University Press.

Reisch, M., & Gambrill, E. (Eds.). (1997). *Social work in the 21st century.* Thousand Oaks, CA: Pine Forge Press.

Reynolds, B. (1951). *Social work and social living.* New York: Citadel.

Richmond, M. (1917). *Social diagnosis.* New York: Russell Sage.

Rivard, J. (1997). *Quick guide to the Internet for social workers.* Boston: Allyn & Bacon.

Roberts, C. (1989). Conflicting professional values in social work and medicine. *Health and Social Work, 13,* 211-218.

Rodgers, H. (1984). Limiting poverty by design: The official measure of poverty. In R. Goldstein & S. Sachs (Eds.), *Applied poverty research* (pp. 49-63). Totowa, NJ: Rowman & Allenhead.

Rooney, R. (1992). *Strategies for working with involuntary clients.* New York: Columbia University Press.

Shulman, L. (1992). *The skills of helping: Individuals, families, and groups.* Itasca, IL: Peacock.

Stack. C., (1974). *All our kin: Strategies for survival in a Black community.* New York: Harper & Row.

Swigonski, M. (1993). Feminist standpoint theory and the questions of social work research. *Affilia, 8,* 171-183.

Walster, E., Walster, W., & Berscheid, E. (1978). *Equity: Theory and research.* Boston: Allyn & Bacon.

Windes, R., & Hastings, H. (1965). *Argumentation and advocacy.* New York: Random House.

Yelaja, S. A. (1982). Values and ethics in the social work profession. In S. A. Yelaja (Ed.), *Ethical issues in social work* (pp. 5-32). Springfield, IL: Charles C Thomas.

INDEX

A

Abbott, A., 73
Aburdene, P., 181
Action log, 169-170
Addams, Jane, 3, 7, 13, 14, 20
Administration of social work, 6
Advocate, social worker as, 20, 35-36
AFDC. *See* Transitional Assistance to
    Needy Families (TANF)
Aging process, witnessing, 175
Assessment, client, 147-153, 163
   strength-based, 151-153

B

Behavioral perspective, 147
Benard, B., 148
Berscheid, E., 149
Biomedical ethics, social workers and,
    65-70
Block, John, 28
Bonnin, Gertrude Simmons, 86, 135-136
   writings, 88-104
Broker, social worker as, 20
Bulhan, H. A., 85

C

Capitalism, 71
Census Bureau, 27
Chapin, R., 148
Charity Organization Society, 3, 7, 13, 71
   "friendly visitor" program, 3
Civil Rights Act, 80
Civil service reform, 7
Community participation, 37
Compton, B., 149
Computers. *See* Internet; Web
Counselor, social worker as, 20
Crow Dog, Mary, 87, 143-144
   writing, 117-134

D

Depression, Great, 3

E

Ecological perspective, 147
"Economy diet plan," 28
Elderly:
   chronic care systems, 181
   future of caring for, 175-177
Empathy, 85, 157
Empowerment, client, 85-87, 147
Estroff, S., 158

F

Fanon, F., 85
Fast, B., 148
Futurists, 181

G

Galaway, B., 149
Gambrill, E., 181
Governmental agencies, 5

H

Hartsock, N., 157
Hastings, H., 19
Haynes, K., 181
Hegel, G. W. F., 85
Hill, Anita, 157
Hoffman, K., 20
Holmes, K., 181
Homophobia, 80
Homosexuality, social work and, 79-81
Horner, W. C., 73
Hoshino, G., 51
Hull House, 3, 13, 14

I

Immigrants, 3
"Individual helping," 13
Informational interview, 14-15
Internet:
   accessing, 52
   hypertext, 53

Internet *(continued)*
  potential, 52
  professional socialization and, 51-56
  URL, 53, 56
  See also Web
Involuntary clients, 75

J

Jamison, Kay Redfield, 86-87, 137-138
  writing, 104-106

K

Karls, L. M., 43
Kelly, Florence, 3, 20

L

Leighninger, L., 71
Licensure, 43-50
  reciprocity, 45
Lowell, Josephine Shaw, 7

M

Mairs, Nancy, 87, 141-142
  writing, 108-117
Malcolm X, 85
Managed care, 181
Marginalized citizens, empowering, 19
Mathis, T. P., 43
McDonald, T., 51
Mediator, social worker as, 20
Medicare services, changes in, 175
Morales, A., 73
Motivation skills, 20

N

Naisbett, J., 181
National Association of Social Workers
  (NASW), 3
  Code of Ethics, 72, 73-74, 80

O

Oppressed persons, 85
  autoppressor, 85
  ego defenses, 85
  resiliency, 86
  See also Bonnin, Gertrude Simmons;
    Crow Dog, Mary; Jamison, Kay
    Redfield; Mairs, Nancy; Wolff,
    Tobias
Organized profession, social work as, 5

P

Participant observation, 158-162
Perlman, H., 149
Persuasive skills, 20
P-FLAG, 80
Popple, P., 71
Population changes, racial/ethnic, 181
Poverty as sin:
  versus nonjudgmentalism, 71
Poverty level, 1997, 27
Poverty-level income, budgeting, 27-34
Poverty line:
  definition, 27
  dialogue/debates, 27, 157
Professional socialization, Internet and,
  51-56
Public issue resolution, 19
Public opinion:
  definition, 19
  sharing, 19
Public policy (local), influencing, 35-40

R

Rapp, C., 148
Reagan presidency, 28
Reisch, M., 181
Relative deprivation, 27
Research, 6. *See also* Participant
  observation
Resource acquisition, 163-172
  barriers, 163-164
  general model, 163
Resource manager, social worker as, 20
Resources:
  community, 163
  formal, 163
  institutional, 163
  personal, 163
Reynolds, Bertha, 20
Richman, Harold, 164
Richmond, Mary, 3, 13
Rivard, J., 51
Roberts, C., 73
Rodgers, H., 27
Rooney, R., 75

S

Sallee, A., 20
School of Social Work, first, 13
Scientific philanthropy, 7
Search engines, 53, 55. *See also* Yahoo
Sheafor, B., 73
Shulman, L., 85
Social Darwinism, 71

Social policy practice, 13
Social reform movement, 13
Social Security system, 181
Social services, privatization of, 181
Social welfare issues, contemporary,
    19-26
Social work:
    career choice, 71
    envision future, 181-183
    history, 3-13
Social work, public perception:
    media, 58
    shaping, 57-64
Social workers:
    authority/power sources, 5
    misconceptions about, 57
    roles, 20
    skill, 6
    social responsibility, 4
Social work method, 5-6
Social work practice:
    knowledge, 5
    philosophical concepts, 4
    purposes, 4
    state regulation, 43-50
    working definition, 3-6
Social work techniques, 6
Stack, C., 158
Standpoint theory, 157
Starr, Ellen Gates, 3
Strategy development skills, 20
Strengths model, Rapp's, 148-150
    principles, 149-150
Swigonski, M., 157

T

Teaching, 6
Toffler, Alvin, 181
Toffler, Heidi, 181
Transitional Assistance to Needy
    Families (TANF), 21, 27

U

U.S. Congress, 175

V

Values:
    clarifying social workers', 65-70
    competence, 74
    dignity/worth of person, 73-74
    human relationships, 74
    integrity, 74, 75
    NASW, 73-74
    religious, 71-75
    service, 73
    social justice, 73
Voluntary incorporated agencies, 5

W

Walster, E., 149
Walster, W., 149
War on poverty, 3
Web:
    addresses, 53
    browsers, 52
    sites, 55
    social work resources, 51-52
Welfare laws, 181
Welfare reform dialogue/debates, 27,
    157, 158
Welfare state, privatization of, 181
Whitbeck, L. B., 73
Windes, R., 19
Wolff, Tobias, 87, 139-140
    writing, 106-108
Women's suffrage, 7
World War I, 3
World War II, 3
World Wide Web. *See* Web

Y

Yahoo, 53